Cambridge Elements ≡

Elements in Shakespeare and Pedagogy
edited by
Liam E. Semler
The University of Sydney
Gillian Woods
Birkbeck College, University of London

TEACHING ENGLISH AS A SECOND LANGUAGE WITH SHAKESPEARE

Fabio Ciambella
Sapienza University of Rome

CAMBRIDGE
UNIVERSITY PRESS

Shaftesbury Road, Cambridge CB2 8EA, United Kingdom

One Liberty Plaza, 20th Floor, New York, NY 10006, USA

477 Williamstown Road, Port Melbourne, VIC 3207, Australia

314–321, 3rd Floor, Plot 3, Splendor Forum, Jasola District Centre,
New Delhi – 110025, India

103 Penang Road, #05–06/07, Visioncrest Commercial, Singapore 238467

Cambridge University Press is part of Cambridge University Press & Assessment,
a department of the University of Cambridge.

We share the University's mission to contribute to society through the pursuit of
education, learning and research at the highest international levels of excellence.

www.cambridge.org
Information on this title: www.cambridge.org/9781009331968

DOI: 10.1017/9781009332002

First published 2024

A catalogue record for this publication is available from the British Library.

ISBN 978-1-009-33196-8 Paperback
ISSN 2632-816X (online)
ISSN 2632-8151 (print)

Teaching English as a Second Language with Shakespeare

Elements in Shakespeare and Pedagogy

DOI: 10.1017/9781009332002
First published online: May 2024

Fabio Ciambella

Sapienza University of Rome

Author for correspondence: Fabio Ciambella, fabio.ciambella@uniroma1.it

ABSTRACT: Teaching pragmatics, that is, language in use, is one of the most difficult and consequently neglected tasks in many English as a Second Language (ESL) classrooms. This Cambridge Element in the Shakespeare and Pedagogy series aims to address a gap in the scholarly debate about Shakespeare and pedagogy, combining pragmatic considerations about how to approach Shakespeare's language today in ESL classes, and practical applications in the shape of ready-made lesson plans for both university and secondary school students. Its originality consists in both its structure and the methodology adopted. Three main sections cover different aspects of pragmatics: performative speech acts, discourse markers, and (im)politeness strategies. Each section is introduced by an overview of the topic and state of the art, and then details are provided about how to approach Shakespeare's plays through a given pragmatic method. Finally, an example of an interactive, ready-made lesson plan is provided.

This Element also has a video abstract: www.Cambridge.org/ESPG_Ciambella

KEYWORDS: English as a Second Language, English pragmatics, content-based language teaching, literature in language education, lesson plan

ISBNs: 9781009331968 (PB), 9781009332002 (OC)
ISSNs: 2632-816X (online), 2632-8151 (print)

Contents

Introduction
Teaching Shakespeare in Language Education – An Example of Content-based Instruction?

Content-based Instruction in the English as a Second Language (ESL) Classroom

Writing his *Teaching Language as Communication* in 1978, when methodologies considering the teaching of language via specific content were gaining momentum, Henry G. Widdowson provided an early, almost poetic and prophetic definition of *Content-based Instruction* (hereafter *CBI*):

> The kind of language course that I envisage is one which deals with a selection of topics taken from the other subjects: simple experiments in physics and chemistry, biological processes in plants and animals, map-drawing, descriptions of historical events and so on. . . . It is easy to see that if such a procedure were adopted, the difficulties associated with the presentation of language use in the classroom would . . . disappear. (16)

CBI, sometimes also called, more specifically, *Content-based Language Teaching* (hereafter *CBLT*),[1] is an umbrella acronym that defines a series of *Second Language Acquisition* (hereafter *SLA*) approaches and methodologies aimed at teaching and learning a *foreign language* (hereafter *FL* or *L2*) with the support of a non-linguistic subject, that is, art, business, science, and so on. The intersections between the FL and the subject matter, and their respective contribution to the creation of successful FL courses, may vary depending on the primary focus of teachers and lecturers. In this Element, I will adopt and adapt Roy Lyster's taxonomy of CBI language courses (2007, 2018) to offer an accurate and solid theoretical framework within which to choose the most suitable CBLT approaches for the teaching of *English as a Second Language* (hereafter *ESL*) through some of William Shakespeare's plays.

---

[1] Although CBI and CBLT present some differences, for the purposes of this Element, these two acronyms are used interchangeably.

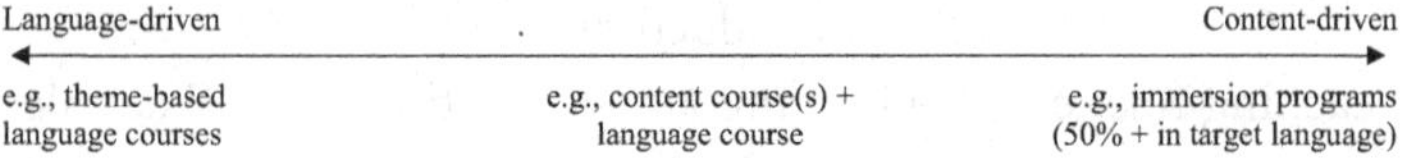

Language-driven   Content-driven

e.g., theme-based   e.g., content course(s) +   e.g., immersion programs
language courses   language course   (50% + in target language)

Figure 1 Lyster's continuum of CBI programmes (adapted from Lyster, 2018: 2).

Lyster's taxonomy of CBI language courses is of particular interest because it consists of 'a range of instructional initiatives [that] can be identified along a continuum' (2018: 2), instead of considering CBLT as a group of rigidly separate methodologies. The two ends of this continuum (see Figure 1) are represented by language-driven and content-driven programmes.

Language-driven courses are 'foreign-language classes that promote target-language development by incorporating a focus on themes or topics with which learners have some familiarity in their L1. ... Such themes provide opportunities for language practice but without high-stakes assessment of students' content knowledge' (2018: 2). This is the case of technical and vocational secondary schools in some African, Asian, and European countries, where ESL syllabi establish the teaching of *English for Special/Specific Purpose(s)* (hereafter *ESP*) to pupils whose expertise and field of studies are quite technical (e.g., agronomy, food and cookery, ICT, etc.).[2] ESP courses are generally delivered by language teachers/experts with varying knowledge of the disciplinary content provided.

The other end of Lyster's continuum is represented by content-driven courses, where L2 acquisition is somehow taken for granted, and embedded in the teaching of specific disciplinary contents. Foreign language becomes the 'medium through' (2018: 3) which content is delivered. Content-driven CBI is typical of immersion programmes in Canada or China, but also of *English as (a) Medium (of) Instruction* (hereafter *EMI*) programmes in internationalised degree courses (see, among others, Pecorari and Malmström, 2018; Bowles and Murphy, 2020; Lasagabaster, 2022) where

---

[2] See, for instance, Harrabi, 2011, for ESP teaching in Tunisian secondary schools, Dewi, 2015 for Indonesian ESP courses, and Ciambella, 2021, for a definition of ESP programmes in Italian secondary schools.

very advanced disciplinary content is delivered exclusively in English, thus taking for granted that students are competent enough to follow classes in this language. In most cases, instructors are content experts with a solid linguistic competence (at least B2+/C1 level).

The middle of the CBI spectrum is occupied by what I have called elsewhere well-balanced courses (Ciambella, 2021: 349), where 'students study one or two subjects in the target language, usually in tandem with a foreign language or language arts class' (Lyster, 2018: 2). *Content and Language Integrated Learning* (hereafter *CLIL*) has been conceived as the well-balanced model par excellence since the acronym was coined by David Marsh and Anne Maljers in 1994. Content and Language Integrated Learning is 'a dual-focused educational approach in which an additional language is used for the learning and teaching of both content and language' (Coyle et al., 2010: 1); therefore, the dual focus on both language and content is fundamental. In the best of all possible worlds, CLIL courses should be delivered by a CLIL team comprising at least one non-linguistic-subject teacher and an English (or FL) teacher. This would guarantee that both language and content receive the same attention and are taught by experts in both fields. In most cases, however, it is the non-linguistic-subject teacher who is entrusted with language teaching in CLIL. Hence the need for training content experts to also become 'language-aware' (He and Lin, 2018: 162), not simply content teachers with *some* Knowledge About Language, as in the case of EMI courses. Being a content teacher with advanced competence in English is not sufficient to being a good CLIL instructor, which is why local governments finance CLIL training courses for non-linguistic-subject teachers, in order to educate students who are global citizens. Figure 2 summarises my integrations to Lyster's CBI continuum.

In this Element, I will move from one end to the other, considering ESP courses taught by language teachers to secondary school students, and EMI programmes taught by content experts to university students. The main linguistic objective will be the teaching of pragmatics, that is, language in a meaningful context, while the principal content goals will range from English literature to the history of the English language. For each of the three sections dedicated to a specific pragmatic strategy, a double

Language-driven ESL courses	(Well-)balanced ESL courses	Content-driven ESL courses
ESP (Language expert teacher)	CLIL (CLIL team, i.e., both language and content teacher, or language-aware content teacher)	EMI (Content expert teacher with advanced competence in English)

Figure 2 Integrations to Lyster's CBI spectrum (adapted from Ciambella, 2021, p. 351).

ready-made lesson plan will be created: one for secondary school students – adopting the ESP framework – and the other for university students – dealing with EMI. Nevertheless, since I have decided to adopt Lyster's model for its fluidity and non-fixedness, both lesson plans can work perfectly in CLIL modules, if adequately adapted to the needs of teachers and lecturers.

Before moving on to consider Shakespeare and his language as a good example of content to be inserted in CBLT programmes, it is worth shedding some light on the legitimacy of literature as content in CBI. Addressing this issue is challenging because literature offers valuable content in content-based programs, yet it is also an integral part of FL curricula. The next section will try to tackle this problem, providing a brief overview of the situation, as well as solutions and suggestions.

Literature as Content in CBI

The role of literature in language courses has been acknowledged in alternating phases,[3] and always with a twofold approach: on the one hand, literature was – and still is – considered the most eminent cultural manifestation of any given nation, state, ethnic group, and so on, thus being a cultural enriching moment within FL programmes. On the other hand,

---

[3] This Element does not deal with a definition of literature, first of all because there is an ongoing, lively debate about the notion of literature and the literary canon, as well as what and how to teach in schools and universities (for issues concerning literary canon(s) and teaching, see, among others, Hall, 2015: 105–06; Aston, 2020). Secondly, since this Element deals only with Shakespeare, it is probably redundant to try and justify his legitimate role in global literature.

language teachers have been underlining its importance as one of the most successful manifestations of historical-natural languages, an achievement to be exploited at its best from a linguistic standpoint, even in terms of imitation and reworking, as will be seen shortly.

According to Susan L. Stern (1985), the implementation of English and American literature in ESL classrooms began almost 100 years ago, between the twilight of the British Empire and the dawn of America as the first world superpower. Alan Duff and Alan Maley (1990: 3) state that from the beginning of the twentieth century to the advent of the Communicative Approach in the 1980s, in ESL classes literature served as a set of source texts to be translated from L2 to L1 and as examples of grammar rules to be learned and then reapplied by students. This teaching method was known as Grammar-Translation. In the 1950s, when communication in FL became central to international scenarios, when more attention needed to be paid to all four basic language skills (reading, writing, listening, and speaking) equally, the Grammar-Translation Method, based on the teaching and learning of classical languages such as Latin and Greek, entered a crisis and fell into disuse, together with the implementation of literature in ESL curricula. According to Geoffrey Hall (2015: 1), this comprised a transition from 'historical dominance' to the 'removal of English literature from its privileged central educational position'. While from the late 1950s to the late 1970s structuralism and functionalism almost ignored the potential of literature in ESL courses, because it was considered old-fashioned and lacking in communicative intent (Llach, 2007; Bobkina, 2014: 249), it was thanks to the influence exerted by such scholars as Jacques Derrida, Colin MacCabe, and Raymond Williams that we 'mov[ed] from literature to cultural studies' (Hall, 2015: 1), thus examining literary texts as manifestations of a given culture, conveyed by a language. This cultural turn, as highlighted by Stern (1985), led to the conclusion that eliminating literature from language syllabi was detrimental for students. The problem remained as to how to integrate literature into the ESL classroom, since the possibilities offered by the Grammar-Translation Method had proved to be unsuccessful and outdated for the ever-growing communicative needs of ESL courses. I must begin by saying that abandoning the Grammar-Translation Method in favour of the Communicative Approach, as shaped by Noam Chomsky, M. A. K. Halliday, Dell Hymes, and others, did and does not mean neglecting the teaching and learning of grammar and translation in *Literature in Language Education* methods (hereafter *LLE*). For instance, recent studies by Hasan Atmaca and Rifat Günday (2016) and Anna Fenn and Rachel McGlynn (2018) propose the teaching and learning of grammar through literary texts, adopting a Communicative Approach.[4]

Several groundbreaking works on language instruction through literature have paved the way for this field. Among them, René Wellek and Austin Warren's seminal *Theory of Literature* (1942; rev. ed. 1956) stands out, recognising literature's dual accessibility through both extrinsic and intrinsic lenses. This involves delving into biographical, social, philosophical, and political contexts that shape a text, as well as exploring its linguistic dimensions. Noteworthy contributions also include Widdowson's influential *Stylistics and the Teaching of Literature* (1975) and Roland Carter and Michael N. Long's *The Web of Words: Exploring Literature through Language* (1987). After these works, Maley (1989) is probably one of the first scholars to explore the communicative potential of literature, thus lucidly 'distinguish[ing] two primary purposes for "literature teaching": 1) the *study* of literature; [and] 2) the *use* of literature as a resource for language learning' (10, Emphases in the original).[5] The study of literature corresponds to what Maley defines as a critical (literary) approach, thus focusing on the literariness of the text, while the use of literature is part of the stylistic approach, with emphasis on a text's linguistic features (11). Maley theorises a third combined approach – which he actually fails to sketch out properly – although LLE classes still tend to separate the two approaches even today, with ESL teachers focusing on either the study or the use of literature in the language classroom, and scholars – especially non-Anglophone ones – seeking an integrated/integrative approach which combines literary criticism and linguistics in the

---

[4] For an overview of the most recent approaches to translation in SLA, see, among others, Alena Ponomareva, 2021, an MA thesis I have co-supervised with my colleague Mary Louise Wardle.

[5] About Maley, Hall commented that he was 'a significant, if not the central "first wave" developer and promoter of classroom pedagogies and materials for literature in communicative language teaching' (2015: 123).

ESL classroom (see, among others, Timucin, 2001; Savvidou, 2004; Divsar and Tahriri, 2009; Dhanapal, 2010; Yimwilai, 2015).

I believe that most of the integrated/integrative approaches that try to combine both the study and the use of literature in ESL classrooms rightly consider literature to be a specific disciplinary content to be implemented in CBLT courses (see, for instance, Brinton et al., 1989; Elyasi, 2013). Literature as content has its own jargon, exactly as do other non-linguistic subjects, thus offering learners the possibility of acquiring specific 'vocabulary, grammar, paragraph structure, interactive communication skills, and types and styles of writing' (Elyasi, 2013: 13), typical micro- and macro-linguistic features of ESP (Gotti, 2003). Moreover, since literature and language are often considered inseparable (Bassnett and Grundy, 1993; Vilches, 2001; Lasagabaster, 2003), in the CBI class, Hall (2015: 4) suggests integrating them as a binomial rather than positioning them as 'two distinct fields'. Given the plethora of approaches to using literature in the CBLT classroom and the range of case studies presented by scholars, as seen thus far, I will attempt to formulate a theoretical framework which combines and integrates most of the models proposed in the scholarly debate around LLE, thus adopting Lyster's taxonomy of CBI courses outlined in the previous paragraph (as revised in Ciambella, 2021), and, moving his continuum back and forth, will also take into account Maley's distinction between the study and the use of literature in the ESL classroom.

Another fundamental point to consider when dealing with CBI is the structure of lesson plans, and even in this case, I will refer to Lyster's studies. I will adopt his *proactive approach* to CBLT, that is, 'pre-planned instruction designed to enable students to notice and to use target language features that might otherwise not be used or even noticed in classroom discourse' (2007: 44). As developed further a few years ago (Lyster, 2018: 15–24), pre-planned instruction comprises a four-phased educational action which corresponds to the traditional tripartition of lesson plans – mainly derived from Lev S. Vygotsky's (1978) and Jerome Bruner's (1983) constructivist theories – into input, scaffolding, and output, as illustrated in Figure 3.

The input phase corresponds to Lyster's *noticing activity* and 'establishes a meaningful context related to content, usually by means of a written or oral text in which target features have been contrived to appear more salient

Focus on content	Noticing activity ⟶	Input
Focus on language	Awareness activity → Guided practice	Scaffolding
Focus on content	Autonomous practice ⟶	Output

Figure 3 The four-phased proactive approach adapted from Lyster (2018: 16).

or more frequent' (2018: 15). Lyster's noticing activity is clearly influenced by Richard Schmidt's noticing hypothesis (1990), albeit largely criticised, according to which input becomes intake (Corder, 1967), that is, input that is processed only if it is noticed, that is, if careful attention is paid to it (Schmidt, 1990: 139). Therefore, the Shakespearean text selected in each lesson plan will be provided in the input/noticing phase to stimulate students' curiosity and let them reflect on the content from the outset. Receptive skills, that is, reading and listening, are generally elicited in the noticing activity phase, to put students at ease without exposing the shiest of them, thus risking raising their affective filter.[6]

Lyster's main innovation is the articulation of the linguistic scaffolding into two sub-phases: *awareness activity* and *guided practice*. Although both phases focus on language, they present some differences. The awareness activity 'encourages students to reflect on and manipulate the target forms in a way that helps them to become more aware of patterns that were high-lighted at the noticing phase [through] rule-discovery tasks, metalinguistic exercises, and opportunities for pattern detection' (Lyster, 2018: 15). The second part of the scaffolding, that is, the guided practice, 'provides opportunities for students to use the grammatical features in a meaningful yet controlled context and to receive corrective feedback in order to develop automaticity and accuracy' (16). In other words, the first part of the scaffolding phase aims at letting students become aware of some

---

[6] As one of the five hypotheses forming Stephen Krashen's monitor model, as seen in the next subsection, the affective filter is a kind of wall that students may or may not build and which prevents them from learning anything. The filter arises because of anxiety, embarrassment, direct and aggressive error correction, and the lack of comprehensible input, among other causes.

linguistic features that are better contextualised and put into practice in the second part.

Lastly, focus on content returns in the *autonomous practice* (the students' output), this time after students have acquired the necessary linguistic structures to work autonomously. In Lyster's words, '[a]utonomous practice requires the use of the target-language features but in a discipline-specific or thematic context. There are fewer constraints, allowing students to use the features in more open-ended ways to develop fluency, motivation, and confidence' (16). It is clear that autonomous practice involves active skills such as writing and speaking and that it refers to Benjamin Bloom's famous revised taxonomy of educational learning objectives (Anderson and Krathwohl, 2001), whose highest cognitive process is 'create', that is, 'a new product . . . coordinated [by] the students' previous learning experiences [which] requires creative thinking' (84–85).

As for activities to be proposed to teach language in the literature class, I will mainly – but not exclusively – refer to Burhanuddin Arafah's list of teaching techniques (2018: 31–34), which I consider a fine synopsis of the most common activities and exercises to be carried out to focus on language in literary texts. The advantages of these techniques are that they are student-centred and can also be implemented using new technologies:

- *Analysing techniques*: 'The centre of attention is the linguistic expressions of the text such as lexical items and phrases' (31). One of the analysing activities proposed by Arafah is Elizabeth B. Ibsen's 'strong lines' (1990): students are required to read a passage from a literary text (a Shakespeare play in our case) and underline expressions they like or that disturb them. Strong lines are shared with the rest of the class, and the most popular becomes the title or the theme of a piece of writing/project work to be carried out individually or in a group.

- *Memorising and producing techniques*: Students 'memorize some lexical items and retell the story by using the words' (32). This is what Nguyen T. T. Thom (2008) called storytelling.

- *Completing techniques*: 'Students are required to complete a story in which some lexical items . . . have been omitted' (33). Gap-filling exercises are clearly the most suitable of these techniques.

- *Constructing techniques*: 'Students are required to construct a story based on key sentences given by the teachers' (33). Maley's 'storylines' falls into this kind of activity (2000). Students are not provided with the passage selected by the teacher at the beginning; only keywords or key sentences, that is, the storylines, are provided. Groups of students invent a story (by writing, uttering, or dramatising it) and share it with the rest of the class. Strong and weak points are discussed, and the best story is selected.
- *Transforming techniques*: 'Students are asked to transform a certain literary work from its original form to another' (34). For instance, a playtext can be transformed into song lyrics or a movie/TV series screenplay.

Shakespeare as CBI: Pros and Cons

As noted in the previous paragraph, Shakespeare's plays will be the literary texts used to teach the pragmatics of the English language in this Element. The next section will investigate the role of pragmatics in ESL courses and the reasons why this volume focuses on this specific level of linguistic analysis. Before doing so, however, it is necessary to understand whether and how a Shakespearean text can be the 'special guest' in a contemporary content-based ESL programme.

We will begin by closely examining whether Shakespeare's works are suitable literary texts to be introduced into the LLE classroom with students of varied ages and levels. To do so, it is necessary to introduce a very well-known concept in SLA theory: Krashen's monitor model, in particular his input hypothesis (1978). According to Krashen, when learners are given an input, the necessary condition is that it be comprehensible. Language acquisition can only occur if students understand the input provided, both quantitatively and qualitatively. As will be seen in the following paragraphs, in this Element, the Shakespearean text will be used as input in the lesson plans proposed; thus, it is crucial that the scenes and lines chosen be comprehensible, especially for non-native secondary school learners, since 'there is plenty of evidence that students' encounters with Shakespeare are often far from the joyous experiences one might hope for, the main culprit being the language' (Murphy et al., 2020: 303).

Few quantitative and qualitative field studies have been conducted so far on ESL or English native secondary school/university students and their actual comprehension of Shakespeare's Early Modern English (see Murphy et al., 2020; Bauer et al., 2022). Results obtained show that the main difficulties stem from outdated grammar – especially syntax – and vocabulary (Crystal, 2012: 10–15), that is, 'overcomplicated sentence structure to say simple things' (Murphy et al., 2020: 303), as one student summarised simplistically yet unequivocally, and lexicosemantic peculiarities such as 'archaisms . . ., items infrequently used in present-day English . . ., colloquial language . . ., malapropisms . . ., culturally contemporary references . . . and false friends' (312).

To make the input comprehensible and to help, in particular, ESL secondary school students, one possible solution is that of grading/scaling down the Shakespearean text, that is, modernising, simplifying, or 'rewording' (to borrow from Jakobson, 1959: 233) it. In technical terms, this process is called intralingual translation and it is quite widespread today in the LLE classroom, although scholars have antithetical opinions about the legitimacy and necessity of such a process. To my knowledge, Paula Blank's position towards intralingual translation of the Shakespearean text and SLA theories is one of the most lucid which summarises previous, long-standing, controversial issues about the modernisation of Shakespeare's Early Modern English and the efficacy this process may have on language acquisition. Starting with the assumption that '[a]s linguists will confirm, Shakespeare's Early Modern English is . . . continuous enough with our own Modern English that we cannot and do not draw formal language boundaries between them' (2018: 15), Blank concludes that translating Shakespeare into contemporary English is not necessary as a ready-made output per se, since 'most modern literary and linguistic scholars still appear convinced by Shakespeare's continued accessibility and proceed as if it is just a matter of providing enough context on sixteenth-century English for contemporary readers to grasp and appreciate his particular uses of it' (16). Moreover, '[w]e are missing an opportunity when we imagine we must either choose Shakespeare's original language . . . or change it for ours' (Blank, 2018: 18).

Actually, I am firmly convinced that it is necessary to adopt one position in this Element and try to answer David Crystal's famous Hamletian question 'To modernize or not to modernize' (2002: 15). Most studies adopt the native speaker perspective, thus raising questions about the modernisation of the Shakespearean text in English as a Native Language classes. In this case, it is rather obvious that rewording Shakespeare's plays is not the best option, especially if one considers the widespread belief in Anglophone countries that 'Shakespeare in other words is not Shakespeare' (Macdonald, 2001: 36). Nevertheless, Sean Murphy et al. (2020) have demonstrated, through an empirical survey conducted on both native speakers and ESL students, that '[d]ifferences between first-language and additional-language speakers were few' and that, what is more, '[b]eing multilingual . . . may confer advantages over monolingual English speakers in understanding Shakespeare' (322). This is true especially in the case of learners whose first language is a romance language, given the influence of Latin on Shakespeare's lexis, which was definitely much more evident than in modern English, for a number of well-known reasons space limitations prevent me from discussing here.[7]

Therefore, I would argue that modernised versions of Shakespeare plays must be considered carefully in this Element. Although spelling modernisation/standardisation is desirable and a very common practice in the ESL classroom (especially in secondary school) nowadays, as pointed out by most scholars (see, among others, Wells, 1984; Holland, 2000; Kidnie, 2021), paraphrased and reworded versions will be avoided for two reasons. First of all, from a purely linguistic perspective, paraphrased texts can alter the understanding and efficacy of some of the pragmatic strategies and devices analysed in this Element. Secondly, from an ideological point of view, ESL students in secondary school are not familiar with intralingual translations even in the literary texts that belong to their own cultural heritage and that they study in their native language. For instance, secondary school students in Italy study Dante's *Divina Commedia* in its original 700-year-old Italian language with notes and glosses to help them

---

[7] See, among others, Nevalainen, 1999, 2006: esp. chapters 3 and 4, 29–58; Culpeper, 2007.

understand archaic morphological and lexical forms, as well as complex, obsolete syntactic structures.

Online resources such as No Fear Shakespeare (by sparknotes.com; see Table 1) or shmoop.com offer the modernised version of not only Early Modern English spelling but also Shakespeare's morphosyntactic structures and vocabulary (effecting a real intralinguistic translation), thus sometimes making the playwright's original language unrecognisable. For instance, here is the intralinguistic translation of the first stanza of *Romeo and Juliet*'s well-known chorus by No Fear Shakespeare:

Therefore, editions of Shakespeare's plays whose spelling has been modernised and which contain an apparatus of editorial notes to enhance an understanding of difficult passages will be adopted as comprehensible input in this Element, as far as lesson plans for secondary school ESL students are concerned (e.g., The New Cambridge Shakespeare series). Intralingual translation, on the other hand, will sometimes be encouraged as a linguistic scaffolding exercise or output. Since the main goal of this Element is to teach/learn pragmatics through Shakespeare, even university students may benefit from scholarly editions of the plays containing modernised spelling only.

Table 1 Intralinguistic translation of *Romeo and Juliet*'s chorus (first stanza) by No Fear Shakespeare (www.sparknotes.com/nofear/shakespeare/romeojuliet/act-1-prologue/).

Original version	Intralinguistic translation
Two households, both alike in dignity (In fair Verona, where we lay our scene), From ancient grudge break to new mutiny, Where civil blood makes civil hands unclean.	In the beautiful city of Verona, where our story takes place, a long-standing hatred between two families erupts into new violence, and citizens stain their hands with the blood of their fellow citizens.

The pedagogy adopted to teach English with Shakespeare in this Element clearly falls into the so-called textual approach, that is, '"close reading" in the classroom, with the teacher translating difficult words and phrases' (Murphy et al., 2020: 304). Since one of the main problems with this approach is that 'the learner is passive' (307), I do not completely exclude either the contextual or the performance approaches[8] listed by Murphy et al. because, as Donatella Montini puts it (2013: 131), Shakespeare plays are speech-purposed texts to be performed, therefore '[m]ore enlightened close reading approach[es]' are needed, which also consider their linguistic, literary, and cultural context, as well as their intrinsic performative nature.

Content, Context, and Co-text: Approaching Pragmatics through Shakespeare

Language experts will not find it surprising that most of the CBLT courses using Shakespeare as content focus mainly on vocabulary, which is certainly the most evident – yet the most obvious and shallow – peculiarity of technical and professional English. Larry Z. Zaroff (2010), for instance, uses Shakespeare to give his premedical students some basic notions of medicine, while John F. Maune (2015) aims to teach the lexis of biochemistry via *Romeo and Juliet*, and Susan Meiki (2022) inserts *Hamlet* in a CLIL module about filmic vocabulary.

In this sense, one of the most recent monographic studies devoted to Shakespeare's language in the ESL classroom is *Teaching Shakespeare to ESL Students* (2017) by Leung C. M. Lau and Wing B. A. Tso. Starting with an overview of the cultural significance and the spread of Shakespeare's plays in China and Hong Kong, Lau and Tso elaborate forty short lessons/activities to implement the study of Shakespeare's language in non-native English educational settings. Thus, most of the activities proposed in the book deal with vocabulary and its interference with other levels of linguistic analysis, for example, pronunciation, morphosyntax, semantics, and pragmatics, the latter

---

[8] 'Contextual approaches ... advocate placing Shakespeare's texts in context, the context of Shakespeare himself, his family, the people he worked with, the society of the time, the political and sociocultural events and so on. ... [Active/performance approaches] concern active methods or performance' (Murphy et al., 2020: 304).

considered especially in relation to figurative language. For example, lesson 2 focuses on onomatopoeic lexical units (5–7), while lesson 4 centres on new words coined by Shakespeare (13–14) and lesson 11 on expanding the students' knowledge of English adjectives (35–36).[9]

Nevertheless, in recent years, there has been a tendency in language pedagogy to move from structuralist-oriented approaches to other methodologies which privilege pragmatics. Scholars have indeed been highlighting the importance of teaching and acquiring pragmatic strategies in the ESL classroom (see, among others, Félix-Brasdefer and Cohen, 2012; Ishihara and Cohen, 2014), with the firm belief that, almost paradoxically, 'pragmatics can be taught in the classroom from beginning levels of language instruction' (Félix-Brasdefer and Cohen, 2012: 650), but, on the other hand, that pragmatic competence 'seem[s] to be difficult for EFL/ESL learners to acquire' (Sharif et al., 2017: 49). Moving from these apparently controversial yet complementary premises, Murphy et al. (2020) reaffirm J. César Félix-Brasdefer and Andrew D. Cohen's point that the level of complexity of the pragmatic strategies taught must be 'congruent with the level of grammatical knowledge (and the level of linguistic proficiency) of the learner' (2012: 659), and corroborate it further by stating that 'the learner is also receiving input on the more traditional areas of linguistic proficiency, such as the grammar and the text, in addition to input on pragmatics. . . . a contextual approach to Shakespeare alone is not sufficient for a complete understanding of the language of a text' (Murphy et al., 2020: 306–07). In other words, both Félix-Brasdefer and Cohen (2012) and Murphy et al. (2020) are referring to the principle of linguistic interfaces, understood as 'the interplay (and . . . the corresponding operations that take place) between different subsystems or core modules of language. The underlying idea is that . . . phonology, prosody, morphology, syntax, semantics and pragmatics are per se free-standing, but actively interact with each other on a number of identifiable levels' (Catasso et al., 2022: 2).

As noted in the previous paragraphs, the core of this Element is divided into three sections, each focusing on the teaching of a specific pragmatic aspect of the English language contextualised in a Shakespeare play

---

[9] It must be pointed out that one of the chapters is entitled 'New Words Coined by Shakespeare', an idea which is usually regarded as a myth nowadays.

belonging to a different genre. Section 1, entitled 'Shakespearean Performative Speech Acts: The Case of *Richard III*', explores how performative speech acts occupy a prominent position as the main rhetorical strategies adopted by Shakespeare's characters. This has been argued convincingly by Keir Elam (2002: 202), Laura Estill (2006), and David Schalkwyk (2019), among others, with reference to how performatives contribute to the performativity/performability of the Shakespearean text. After investigating the advantages offered by this pragmatic approach to the teaching of Shakespeare's language in ESL classes, a lesson plan for *Richard III* is presented. This history play is considered one of the most pragmatic-centred of all Shakespeare's plays (see Malouf, 2017; Hamamra, 2019). Given the strong connection between performative speech acts and matters of performativity/performability, oral skills will be privileged in the output. In Lesson Plan 1, students will be asked to identify and distinguish performative speech acts in the play: university students will use different taxonomies elaborated by pragmaticians, while secondary school students will be introduced to the most common ones. Secondary school students will be instructed in using online tools such as the Cambridge Dictionary (available at https://dictionary.cambridge.org) or the Merriam-Webster Dictionary (available at www.merriam-webster.com) in order to investigate which speech acts are still used in contemporary English and which sound obsolete and need to be replaced by current equivalent expressions. They will also be helped by the footnotes in the New Cambridge edition of *Richard III* and in the modernised versions of the play available online (e.g., Shmoop, Sparknotes, etc.). Creative spoken outputs will be encouraged in the form of modernised versions of *Richard III*'s dialogues, role play activities highlighting similarities and differences between early modern and contemporary performative speech acts (e.g., interviews with characters from the play), or debates, a methodology that is spreading at an incredible pace in schools and universities today (see Cinganotto, 2019).

Section 2 is entitled 'Teaching Shakespearean Discourse Markers with *Romeo and Juliet*'. *Discourse markers* (hereafter DMs) are one of the most important structures ESL students should acquire to produce coherent and cohesive written outputs. Drawing on studies about DMs in Early Modern

English, this section presents some examples of Shakespearean DMs and their influence on contemporary English. *Romeo and Juliet* will be considered a suitable case study for a lesson plan on Shakespeare's DMs, due to its great popularity among ESL students and its richness in these pragmatic devices (as highlighted in Busse and Busse, 2012). In Lesson Plan 2, both secondary school and university students are asked to identify them in the tragedy and contextualise them in the different situations in which they are inserted. Written skills will be privileged as output: for instance, secondary school students will be instructed to rewrite some dialogues as WhatsApp conversations/email exchanges, thus modernising some DMs, while university students will be required to write a piece of creative writing in order to reproduce such pragmatic devices in different, creative contexts (e.g., 'Write Friar Lawrence's letter to Romeo using as many discourse markers as possible to make it pragmatically salient. Will you be able to change the tragic events that follow Romeo's exile?').

Section 3, '(Im)polite Shakespeare in *The Taming of the Shrew*', draws mainly on Penelope Brown and Stephen C. Levinson's (1978/87) and Jonathan Culpeper's (1996, 2011a, 2011b, 2018) taxonomies of (im)politeness, on the one hand, and Keith Allan and Kate Burridge's (2006) analysis of forbidden words, on the other, to analyse theoretical aspects connected with taboo language and insults in Early Modern and contemporary English. Vulgar language is still considered a taboo in many education environments, yet it represents one of the most vivid and productive parts of any natural language. In Section 3, I argue that taboo language can be implemented safely in ESL courses to educate citizens who refine their awareness of the pragmatic force that offences and insults have in contemporary society, and how risky they are in certain situations. Among Shakespeare's comedies, *The Taming of the Shrew* is certainly one of the most appropriate for a lesson plan (see Lesson Plan 3), about Shakespearean taboo language (Del Villano, 2018: 137–72), as taboo expressions and insults pervade the play. Both written and oral outputs will be elicited. For example, both secondary school pupils and university students will work on written scripts or song lyrics for short TikTok videos or longer vlogs (Video blogs), respectively, interpreting some characters of *The Shrew* and trying to exploit the vividness of taboo language or avoiding vulgar expressions by paraphrasing them.

1 Shakespearean Performative Speech Acts: The Case of *Richard III*

Speech Act Theory: A Brief Overview

Any introduction to English traditional speech act theory, that is, 'a theory that a verbal utterance should be considered in terms of the intention of the speaker to bring about a particular result by making it and not solely as a statement with intrinsic meaning or reference' (Oxford English Dictionary, hereafter *OED*), should start considering the pivotal and pioneering studies of the philosopher of language J. L. Austin and his disciple John R. Searle, who, around the 1950s and 1970s, laid the foundations for the discipline of pragmatic acts. I should begin by saying that Austin and Searle's speech act theory is primarily interactional and thus implies the existence of a speaker (hereby called S) and a hearer (H) whose roles are interchangeable according to turn-taking rules (see Sacks et al., 1974, for a foundational study about turn-taking and conversation analysis). In this sense, the Shakespearean theatre, and theatrical texts in general, offer a rich field of research for the application of such theories, given their intrinsic dialogic nature: even monologues and soliloquies presuppose the existence of a hearer, that is, the audience. As Saltz asserted, the actors' performance onstage 'is committed to the real performance of illocutionary acts[10] [that] transforms whatever social reality the actors choose to portray into a living reality, at least for the duration of the performance' (2000: 77).

The *OED* definition given at the beginning of this section introduces the notion of utterance, a notion which deserves attention in pragmatics. Generally speaking, an utterance is a group of words, communicating the S's intentions, interrupted only by pauses, thus referring to the concrete oral use of a language, while a sentence is an abstract and ideal concept whose components are usually held together by grammar rules. In other words, '[w]hereas the term "sentence" refers to a formal, structural unit, the term "utterance" refers to a realisation of a speaker's communicative intention: what a speaker says at a given point in time at a given location with a given

---

[10] For a definition of illocutionary acts, see later in this section.

intention' (Plag et al., 2015: 185). More specifically, in pragmatics, 'sentences can ... be realised as many different utterances' (Culpeper and Haugh, 2014: 155), that is, the usage of language and the S's intentions determine the passage from sentences to utterances.[11] In this section, we will examine utterances, rather than sentences, but an issue arises when the text considered – *Richard III* in this case – is written on a page. Nevertheless, given the speech-purposed nature of dramatic texts (Jucker, 1995, 2006; Culpeper and Kytö, 2010: 17; Montini, 2013: 131), I will treat them as representations of spoken language.

One fundamental principle theorised by Austin (1962: esp. lecture VIII, 92–107) is the distinction between the locutionary, illocutionary, and perlocutionary force that a speech act possesses and that determines both the S's intentions and the H's understanding and/or implicatures:[12]

- Locutionary force: The simple production of a speech act in its linguistic form with sense and reference (e.g., 'Nice weather today, innit?')
- Illocutionary force: The act/intention given by the S to the utterance (in the previous example, if the weather is not fine, the S may be ironic about his/her statement, thus communicating exactly the opposite of the locutionary act)
- Perlocutionary force: The effects produced on the H (with reference to the same example, the H may understand the S's irony or, in case (s)he does not share the same situational context, may interpret the sense of the statement literally, as if the weather were really fine).

---

[11] The difference between sentence and utterance may well be part of the broader traditional Saussurian distinction between langue (the abstract rules and conventions of a language) and parole (the concrete realisation of these rules and conventions by speakers of a community).

[12] Explicitly defined for the first time by another noted philosopher of language/ pragmatician, H. Paul Grice (1968), a conversational implicature is '[t]he act or an instance of (intentionally) implying a meaning which can be inferred from an utterance in conjunction with its conversational or semantic context, but is neither explicitly expressed nor logically entailed by the statement itself; a meaning that is implied contextually, but is neither entailed logically nor stated explicitly' (*OED*, n.).

In this example, it is clear that the S needs to share some conditions with the H in order for his/her statement to obtain the desired effects, that is, in order to minimise the distance between illocution and perlocution. Austin (1962: 14) and Searle (1969: 66–67) devoted ample space to defining what they called felicity or felicitous conditions, that is, shared conditions between S and H that enable the success of the performative force of an utterance. These conditions, labelled by Yule (1996: 50), can be summarised as follows:

- General condition: The H must understand the basic linguistic features of an utterance, that is, its phonological, morphosyntactic, and semantic characteristics.
- Content condition: The semantic content of the utterance must be clearly rendered by the S.
- Preparatory condition: There are some basic prerequisites in order for the illocutionary force of utterance to be successfully performed. Each kind of speech act has its own preparatory conditions. For example, requests are usually imposed on those people whom we believe are able to fulfil them (e.g., one would not usually ask a three-year-old child to lift a heavy piece of furniture while moving house).
- Sincerity condition: The S must truly want to carry out the act.
- Essential condition: Both S and H should count on the actual possibility that the speech act can be put into practice. For instance, when the S invites the H out for coffee, the S must regard his/her act as a proper invitation and the H as well, not as a joke or something else.

Therefore, if all of these conditions (or even some of them) are present in a conversation, the H should be able to first understand the semantic meaning of an utterance, and then its pragmatic meaning, that is, what the S's intentions are. This process of discovering the pragmatic meaning of an utterance is called inferencing.[13] Inferences are facilitated by different kinds of knowledge (Plag et al., 2015: 197–200):

---

[13] For a thorough analysis of the differences and similarities between such notions as implicature and inference, see Terkourafi, 2021.

- Situational knowledge or knowledge of the situational context of an utterance (objects present, mimic, posture, etc.)
- Interpersonal knowledge: The level of reciprocal knowledge both S and H share (do they know each other? Are they friends?)
- World knowledge:[14] Knowledge of the things and spaces that surround both S and H in the world (if they talk about a piston rod, for example, do they both know what it is?)
- Co-textual knowledge: Knowledge of the co-text, that is, of the context of the surrounding text, what they have said before (this is the out-and-out linguistic knowledge they must both possess).

Austin distinguishes between two main kinds of speech acts: performative and constative. Performative speech acts are used by the S to undertake a certain action or to make it be undertaken by the H. Conversely, the S utters a constative speech act when (s)he simply makes a statement that can be either true or false. Performatives are sometimes introduced by performative verbs, that is, a verb that prepares the H for the content of the utterance by anticipating its illocutionary force. These kinds of performatives introduced by a performative verb are called explicit performatives (e.g., 'Mum, I assure you I will clean my room tomorrow'), while implicit performatives are not introduced by any performative verb (e.g., 'I will clean my room tomorrow, mum').

After distinguishing between performatives and constatives, Austin draws a very careful, non-definitive, and 'troublesome' (1962: 151) taxonomy of speech acts, which he defines not as such, but as '[c]lasses of utterance, classified according to their illocutionary force' (1962: 150). The five classes are as follows:

- Verdictives: Uttering a judgement (e.g., 'estimate, reckoning, or appraisal')
- Exercitives: Exercising power (e.g., 'appointing, voting, ordering, urging, advising, warning')
- Commissives: Obliging or declaring intentions (e.g., 'declarations, or announcements of intentions, . . . promises, . . . espousals')

---

[14] Interpersonal and world knowledge are also referred together as background knowledge.

- Behabitives: Expressing S's attitudes or feelings (e.g., 'apologizing, congratulating, commending, condoling, cursing, and challenging')
- Expositives: Clarifying reasons, argument, or communication (e.g., '"I reply", "I argue", "I concede", "I illustrate", "I postulate"') (Austin, 1962: 150–51).

Searle (1969) moved from Austin's premises and developed a more detailed taxonomy of speech acts. To Searle's taxonomy, I will add Geoffrey N. Leech's category of rogatives (1983), as presented also by Culpeper and Michael Haugh (2014: 164):

- Assertives or representatives: The S asserts a state of affairs as (s)he sees it (affirming, describing, stating, etc.)
- Commissives: The S is committed to certain actions (offering, promising, threatening, etc.)
- Declarations: The S changes the state of affairs by declaring something (naming, baptising, pleading, sentencing, etc.)
- Directives: The H is directed by the S to perform certain actions (commanding, ordering, requesting, suggesting, etc.)
- Expressives: The S expresses his/her feelings (apologising, complimenting, congratulating, insulting,[15] thanking, etc.)
- Rogatives: The S questions the H about something (asking, querying, questioning, etc.).

Not all kinds of utterances may be inserted in Austin's, Searle's, or Leech's taxonomy, but most of the ones they identified and classified will be considered in the following paragraphs when analysing speech acts in *Richard III*.

Speech Acts and Early Modern English: A Multidisciplinary Field of Research

Marcella Bertuccelli Papi's 'impertinent question . . . "is a diachronic speech act theory possible?"', which gives the title to her breakthrough article about speech acts and their historical pragmatic investigation (2000: 57), can

---

[15] Insults are analysed in Section 3 of this Element.

be considered the official beginning of diachronic speech act theory as we know it today, although some foundations for the discipline had already been laid by Brigitte Schlieben-Lange (1976, 1983), Andreas H. Jucker (1995), and Leslie K. Arnovik (1999). One of the main problems with the diachronic perspective regarding speech act theory is, according to Bertuccelli Papi, 'consistent theoretical divergencies in synchronic speech act analysis' (2000: 57); hence, it is difficult to elaborate a solid theoretical framework 'whose coordinates are context-specific, culture-specific, and time-specific' (64). In other words, the 'main divergencies' (58)[16] concerning the analysis of speech acts in contemporary discourse are even more evident when trying to explore historical varieties of language with pragmatic frameworks elaborated for contemporary English. To borrow a very well-known metaphor used by Bertuccelli Papi, '[w]e may climb a mountain with various types of equipment, and starting from any of its slopes, but we need be aware that they may be slippery and treacherous in various ways. And the history of language is a very difficult mountain to climb' (64).

In addition, echoing Arnovik's statement that '[w]hen we widen our lens to view formal, semantic, syntactic, pragmatic, and cultural factors altogether a labyrinthine tangle confronts us' (1999: 1), Jucker and Irma Taavitsainen affirm that '[w]hile we know a lot about the development of sounds and sound patterns, and the structure of words, phrases and sentences, we still know very little about how speakers use words and sentences to communicate' (2008: 1). In this sense, I would argue, the drama of Shakespeare and his contemporaries offers a prime example of how people used words in context in the Early Modern English period, given the plays' speech-purposed characteristics, yet considering the fictional nature of their language.

Despite the difficulties in adapting contemporary-oriented pragmatic frameworks of speech act theory to historical varieties of language, in the

---

[16] According to Bertuccelli Papi, divergencies concern '[p]ropositional meaning vs. illocutionary meaning, standard vs. occasional meaning, universality vs. culture-boundedness, directness vs. indirectness, conventionality vs. inferentiality, society vs. cognition, the relation between utterance form and illocutionary structure, the role of the context, speech act typology' (2000: 58).

last two decades, pragmaticians have been studying the various historical contexts in which the English language has been employed, thus 'giv[ing] instructive and comprehensive overviews of recent diachronic research on speech acts in the history of the English language' (Kohnen, 2015: 52). In order to justify and corroborate diachronic speech act frameworks, Jucker and Taavitsainen (2008: 3–4) appeal to the Uniformitarian principle,[17] which establishes connections and replicable patterns of language among different periods of time, spaces, and contexts. As William Labov notes, 'the forces operating to produce linguistic change today are of the same kind and order of magnitude as those which operated five or ten thousand years ago' (1972: 275). In this sense, Laurel J. Brinton, analysing occurrences of 'I mean' from Early Modern to contemporary English using corpus-based methods (hence working on big data), asserts that 'pragmatic meaning works uniformly over periods and societies' (2007: 40). Adopting this perspective, Jucker and Taavistainen conclude that 'even pragmatic phenomena like speech acts seem to repeat the basic patterns in slightly modified forms over the course of history' and reassure their reader that '[p]eople and human behaviour cannot have changed so much in the course of years, decades, and centuries'[18] (2008: 4). Nevertheless, what is crucial to understand, I believe, is exactly what we mean by 'slightly modified forms' and how to identify them. Elizabeth C. Traugott and Richard B. Dasher (2002), for instance, suggest looking at semantic changes/shifts of single words (e.g., the verb 'to curse', as we will see in *Richard III*) to better carry out and understand inferences. Instead of concentrating on purely intralinguistic factors, Jucker and Taavitsainen insist on contextual factors: '[i]n speech act studies we look at social action through fragments: instances of an activity type. In this activity, the context gives us clues on how to

---

[17] Born in the field of geology (see *Principles of Geology*, 1830–33, by Sir Charles Lyell), the Principle of Uniformity had already been adopted by linguists by the end of the nineteenth century. One of the most eminent linguists advocating for the Uniformitarian principle was Labov (1972), the founder of sociolinguistics.

[18] Although this is not the proper space in which to discuss this topic, it is interesting to consider what anthropologists, ethnographers, and sociologists think about Jucker and Taavitsainen's latter observation.

understand and interpret the speech act. The frame of the action and the response are important (cf. cognitive approaches)' (2008: 5). Their framework will be discussed in more detail in Section 3. Nevertheless, two considerations are worth being outlined here:

1. Jucker and Taavitsainen take for granted that the taxonomy of speech acts elaborated by Searle is also valid for historical varieties of English. As we will see, the 'slightly modified forms' mainly concern not only semantic changes, as stated by Traugott and Dasher (2002), but also morphosyntactic and lexical variations and their interfaces with pragmatics.

2. The kinds of analyses presented thus far are mainly qualitative and can consider limited groups of words that underwent transformations in restricted groups of texts. Single case studies must be considered, each contributing to adding bricks to the wall of a broader perspective on diachronic speech act theory.

More recently, corpus-based approaches to pragmatics have tried to shed further light on diachronic speech act theory, thus broadening the perspectives offered by previous studies by referring to 'huge amounts of data, quick access, replicability, and advances in corpus design' (Kohnen, 2015: 52). The intent of these studies (see, among others, Kohnen, 2004, 2008; Taavitsainen et al., 2015) is mainly that of providing more general frameworks of historical speech act theory, based not on single or restricted groups of case studies, but on large historical corpora. Among these frameworks, it is worth mentioning Martin Weisser's DART taxonomy/scheme (Dialogue Annotation and Research Tool, latest version n. 3.0; see Weisser 2016, 2018, 2019, 2020), which expands Austin's and Searle's classifications to 160 speech acts, plus two additional categories, that is, unclassifiable and uninterpretable. Unfortunately, given its complexity and the criticism it has received (see, for instance, Brosa Rodríguez, 2021: 43; Verdonik, 2022), the DART taxonomy is not dealt with in this volume. Therefore, Searle's revision of Austin's classification will be adopted to analyse speech acts in *Richard III*, even considering the pedagogical (hence not exclusively research-oriented) aim of the lesson plans presented in the following sections. Nevertheless, as noted by Thomas Kohnen, whatever the methodology followed to study diachronic speech acts, scholars still adopt form-to-mapping approaches, looking for case studies and single/limited empirical data to return to general frameworks:

> Researchers may just collect illustrative examples of a particular speech act which they consider typical manifestations (for example, in a particular period of the English language). Or they may start with (a selection of) specific manifestations that can be defined in terms of form (for example, explicit performatives or imperatives) and systematically search for them in diachronic corpora throughout the history of English. (2015: 54)

For example, looking at the most recurrent 3-grams (strings of three words) with the aid of corpus linguistics methods, Culpeper (2007: 64) noticed that the grammatical frame 1ST PERSON PRONOUN + PERFORMATIVE VERB + 2ND PERSON PRONOUN is extremely widespread in Shakespeare's plays. Expressions such as '*I thank you*, *I warrant you*, *I assure you*, *I beseech you*, *I entreat you*, [and above all] *I pray you*' (Culpeper and Haugh, 2014: 159, Emphasis in the original) are found in abundance and can be considered explicit performatives, that is, speech acts presented by a performative verb that introduces the illocutionary force of the act itself. These and other acts will be analysed and contextualised within the plot of *Richard III* in the next subsection, with particular reference to the effects they have on the H.

Speech Acts in Richard III

Most of the studies devoted to the analysis of speech acts in Shakespeare's *Richard III* focus on curses uttered by female characters – especially Anne and Margaret – and the effects they produce, or, at least, aim to produce (see, among others, Ghezzi Jr., 2024). When dealing with cursing women in early modern England, a few considerations must be advanced. First of all, as summarised by Stephen Orgel (1996), chastity and silence were the most appreciated virtues in women on the Early Modern English stage, with female characters struggling to be heard but most often silenced by their male counterparts. For this reason, 'cursing women were known to transgress the border of the feminine virtue of silence' (Hamamra, 2019: 117). Resistance to silence was clearly manifested in language, that is, pragmatic force. Judith Butler (1999: 25) argues convincingly that resistance to silence helps the female characters' identity be construed in the play, and Alexandra Malouf underlines that language – especially the language of curses – is actually 'the[ir] primary source of power . . . in *Richard III*' (2017: 65),[19] 'a substitute for political action', as argued by Keith Thomas (1971: 509). The question here is to understand whether female characters in the play have actual power. On the other hand, male characters tend to be associated with action, although their use of language is usually the manifestation of their political and legal power, something that Richard definitely possesses in the play and that overcomes his physical deformity and limitations to act as a healthy king.

The second aspect to consider when focusing on curses is the 'association with witchcraft' (Malouf, 2017: 66) of female characters who curse. Drawing from a corpus of 'learned treatises containing narratives of witchcraft events, and . . . sets of courtroom witness dispositions', Culpeper and Elena Semino (2000: 2) observed that *curse* and *wish* were the two most common performative verbs associated with witchcraft between the late-sixteenth and mid-seventeenth century, used 'in the "modern" sense of simply expressing a desire that something negative happens to the target' (7). Moreover, '[i]n the witchcraft context, . . . these two verbs were used to refer to a speech act which was believed to result inevitably in some misfortune falling on the target' (7). I would argue that in *Richard III* both connotations are used by Shakespeare's characters, with an evident preponderance of women. Examining the occurrences and collocations of the lemmas *curse* and *wish*[20] – and their lexical forms – in *Richard III* helps confirm Culpeper and Semino's findings. Tables 2 and 3

---

[19] Most of the studies introduced in this section consider the Folio version of the play (1623), and not the quarto version of 1597.

[20] Although Culpeper and Semino focused on *curse* and *wish* as performative verbs, in this section, I will also consider other grammar classes (e.g., *curse* and *wish* as nouns).

illustrate the absolute frequency of the lemmas sought for, the characters who utter them, and, in some cases, important information about their collocational patterning.[21]

Some easy statistics are worth presenting before analysing the Tables 2 and 3. *Curse* has forty-four occurrences, twenty-seven of which (61 per cent) are in women's speeches and seventeen (39 per cent) in men's utterances. When looking at the collocational patterning, however, we discover that most of the hits of *curse* in male speeches actually refer to curses uttered by female characters (Anne and Margaret in particular) through possessives such as 'thy', 'her', 'Margaret's', and so on. Similarly, *wish* has twelve occurrences, seven of them (58 per cent) in women's speeches and five (42 per cent) in men's utterances. It is important to note that in both cases, Richard is semantically ambiguous. In contrast to male characters like Hastings, Rivers, or Buckingham, who do not employ *curse* and *wish* in a manner intended to bring about negative consequences for a specific target, as societal norms dictated for men, Richard stands out. He utilises these linguistic elements with malicious intent, exemplified by his expression 'I wish the bastards dead' (4.2.19). This linguistic approach aligns with the idea of Richard embodying 'various, often opposing, gendered positions' (Malouf, 2017: 66), underscoring the complexity of his character even in a linguistic context. If one concurs with Juliet Dusinberre's assertion that '[i]n Shakespeare's plays men are conscious of being effeminized if their only weapons are words' (1996: xxvii), then Richard emerges as deliberately ambiguous. He engages in combat with women using their own verbal weapons, a strategy influenced by both his deformity, which hinders him from 'strutting before a wanton ambling nymph' (1.1.17), and his inability to 'prove himself a lover' (1.1.28) in the conventional manner that other men employ. In this sense, although most critics affirm that 'cursing in *Richard III* in inherently feminine' (Hamamra, 2019: 118) and that Richard's rhetorical abilities are so advanced that he manages 'to silence women's voices and to curtail the

---

[21] The analysis has been conducted using the corpus linguistics software #Lancsbox. Due to space limitations, only the results will be provided and discussed, without describing the methodology adopted and its process(es).

Table 2 Occurrences and collocational patterning of the lemma *curse*.

Character	Hits	Collocational patterning
(Lady) Anne	10	
(Queen) Margaret	8	
Richard	8	• 'be not so cursed' (1.2.49)[22] – to Anne, meaning 'shrewish', with a pun on 'curse' (72) • 'blessings for curses' (1.2.69) – referred to Anne • 'Curse not thyself' (1.2.137) – referred to Anne • 'With curses in her mouth' (1.2.236) – referred to Anne
(Queen) Elizabeth	5	
Duchess (of York)	4	
(Lord) Hastings	3	• 'thy frantic curse' (1.3.247) – referred to Margaret • 'her curses' (1.3.304) – referred to Margaret • 'thy heavy curse' (3.4.91) – referred to Margaret
(Earl) Rivers	3	• 'Then cursed she Hastings, then cursed she Buckingham, / Then cursed she Richard' (3.3.16–17) – referred to Margaret
(Duke of) Buckingham	2	• 'curses never pass / The lips of those that breathe them in the air' (1.3.285–86) – referred to Margaret's 'my curse' (1.3.284) • 'Margaret's curse' (5.1.25)
(Lord) Grey	1	• 'Margaret's curse' (3.3.14)

22 All quotations from *Richard III* are taken from the New Cambridge edition, edited by Janis Lull. Only act, scene, and line numbers will be quoted in the main text. See references for more details. As this edition relies on the Folio text of the play, I will exclusively examine speech acts as they appear in the 1623 version.

Table 3 Occurrences and collocational patterning of the lemma *wish*.

Character	Hits	Collocational patterning
Anne	3	
Richard	3	
Buckingham	2	'This is the day that, in King Edward's time, / I wished might fall on me, when I was found / False to his children or his wife's allies. / This is the day wherein I wished to fall / By the false faith of him whom most I trusted' (5.1.12–17).
Elizabeth	2	
Margaret	2	

political threat they pose to his ruthless domination' (123) by using their own weapons, I prefer to consider the scenes that stage the dialogues between Richard, Anne, and Margaret as a sort of witchcraft battle of curses where gender roles are blended and flattened. Margaret, widow of Richard's cousin, the late King Henry VI, 'is the vocal force of divine retribution against Richard's blasphemous actions' (123) and 'a prophetess' (1.3.301). Her curses are divine, since she continually invokes God's intervention to punish Richard who 'is unsuccessful in his attempt to turn her curse back upon her' (Hamamra, 2019: 124). In the end, in fact, her curses prove to be prophetic: 'the bloody dog is dead' (5.5.2), proclaims Richmond at Bosworth after killing Richard and before being crowned King Henry VII, the first Tudor monarch.

Conversely, Anne's curses are ineffective. Widow of Edward, the only son of King Henry VI, and now Queen of England after marrying Richard, she curses her husband as he is responsible for the deaths of her late father-in-law and husband. As noted by Paige M. Reynolds, her curses have nothing divine, but 'maintain the memory of the dead' (2008: 20). Unlike Margaret, whose curses are recognised as having been fulfilled in the end by all characters, Anne is annihilated by Richard's 'deceptive rhetorical power to combat the perlocutionary effects of [her] curses' (Hamamra, 2019: 122), and when she has the chance to kill Richard with a sword that he himself hands her, she is incapable of overstepping 'the confines of her female body' (Charnes, 1993: 46) by executing him with 'a phallic weapon' (Hamamra, 2019: 122).

However, one may ask, what kind of speech act is curses? As seen in the previous paragraph, from the standpoint of illocution, Austin lists curses under the category of behabitives, that is, expressing the S's attitudes and feelings, together with other (re)actions: 'apologizing, congratulating, commending, condoling, . . . and challenging' (1962: 151). He then specifies that behabitives 'include the . . . reaction to other people's behaviour and fortunes, and of attitudes and expression of attitudes to someone's past conduct or imminent conduct' (159). Nevertheless, Culpeper and Semino point out that the use of *curse* and *wish* in witchcraft narratives (and, I might add, in *Richard III* as well) can be better ascribed to a category 'that could . . . do justice to speech acts that cause (or are believed to cause) a change in the world' (2000: 9). Therefore, they believe that Austin's exercitives are a better category to accommodate curses. Exercitives are speech acts which indicate the exercise of power by the S – for example, 'appointing, voting, ordering, urging, advising, warning' (Austin, 1962: 150) – 'the giving of a decision in favour or against a[n] ... action ...; [a] decision that something is to be so, as distinct from a judgment that it is so' (154). Arguing that 'exercitives appear to be a rather miscellaneous category, which does not fully capture the essence of speech act attributed to the witch', Culpeper and Semino (2000: 9) refer to Searle's taxonomy and distinguish between early modern and contemporary curses, thus acknowledging a semantic and pragmatic change in the use of the language of curses. As summarised in Culpeper and Haugh, while '[t]oday cursing is more about expressing ill feelings, being bad-tempered and using taboo language [and] fits in the expressive group', in Early Modern English '[c]urses were a type of declaration [since] witches' words had the power to change the world (e.g., cause sickness and death)' (2014: 167). Moreover, according to Searle's taxonomy, declarations have the power to change the state of affairs by declaring something. In this sense, Margaret's curses in *Richard III* have this power, while Anne's are powerless.

Before focusing on the lesson plan, it is worth glancing at Ramie Targoff's study (2002) of *amen* as a speech act in *Richard III*. Considered a 'devotional performative' (63), *amen* is also an implicit performative for Austin, that is, a speech act 'which affirm[s] a prior utterance' (65). Bridget G. Upton maintains that in the Gospels *amen* is understood as 'a form of closure [and] conforms to the category of declaratives .... Such an act requires ... that the speaker has sufficient authority to utter it, and to bring about the desired perlocutionary effect, in this case, of declaring the narrative to be both finished and in some sense true' (2006: 169–70). It is with this religious sense that *amen* is used in *Richard III*, the only Shakespeare play that ends with *amen*, here the last word uttered by the new crowned King Henry VII, founder of the Tudor dynasty. For example, when at 2.2.107–08, Richard's mother, the Duchess of York, salutes her son with a blessing ('God bless thee and put thy meekness in thy breast, / Love, charity, obedience, and true duty'), he answers 'Amen' (109) to 'seal or confirm' (Targoff, 2002: 62) his mother's utterance, adding in an aside that a mother should also wish her son a long life and reign – something the

Duchess does not do. Similarly, when Richard is crowned in 3.7, the citizens answer 'Amen' (239) to Buckingham's blessing 'Long live King Richard, England's worthy king' (238). Nevertheless, as highlighted earlier, the most significant *amens* resound from the lips of Richmond upon his coronation as King Henry VII: 'Great God of heaven, say Amen to all! . . . What traitor hears me, and says not amen? . . . peace lives again: / That she may long live here, God say amen!' (5.5.8–41). This declarative speech act serves as a potent expression of approval and consent, carrying weight not only in religious contexts but also in the realm of political transactions, as emphasised by Targoff (2002: 61). In this last scene, *amen* seals the pact between God and the new-born sacred dynasty Shakespeare's queen (Elizabeth I) belonged to by declaring and affirming that Henry VII, Elizabeth's grandfather, is the rightful king of England.

Lesson Plan 1

The lesson plan I have created for speech acts in *Richard III* has a dual aim: on the one hand, to make students (both at secondary school and university levels) reflect upon various kinds of speech acts in the play, hence not only curses and *amen*, and on the other hand, to focus on female characters and their complex and multifaceted use of speech acts, especially when feelings are expressed, that is, when expressives are employed. In fact, on the early modern stage, women are often associated with emotions, this being seen as a weak trait, as most scholars acknowledge (see, among others, Findlay, 2010: 470; Novy, 2013: 77; Vaught, 2008: 98).

Noticing Activity (Input)

Secondary School

During the input phase, all students familiarise themselves with the lines selected from the Shakespearean text (4.1.32–95). The teacher may introduce *Richard III*'s plot and main themes to secondary school students, while university students should know the play in advance by reading it and/or Lull's introduction to The New Cambridge Shakespeare edition (2009: 1–51).

STANLEY. *[To Anne]* Come, madam, you must straight to Westminster,
There to be crowned Richard's royal queen.
ELIZABETH. Ah, cut my lace asunder,
That my pent heart may have some scope to beat,
Or else I swoon with this dead-killing news.
ANNE. Despiteful tidings. Oh, unpleasing news.
... DUCHESS. O ill-dispersing wind of misery.
O my accursed womb, the bed of death.
A cockatrice hast thou hatched to the world,
Whose unavoided eye is murderous.
... ANNE. ... I in all unwillingness will go.
Oh, would to God that the inclusive verge
Of golden metal that must round my brow
Were red-hot steel, to sear me to the brains.
Anointed let me be with deadly venom
And die ere men can say 'God save the queen'.
ELIZABETH. Go, go, poor soul, I envy not thy glory.
To feed my humour, wish thyself no harm.
ANNE. No? Why? When he that is my husband now
Came to me, as I followed Henry's corpse,
When scarce the blood was well washed from his hands
Which issued from my other angel husband
And that dead saint which then I weeping followed,
Oh, when, I say, I looked on Richard's face,
This was my wish: 'Be thou', quoth I, 'accursed,
For making me, so young, so old a widow!' ...
ELIZABETH. Poor heart, adieu; I pity thy complaining.
ANNE. No more than from my soul I mourn for yours.
ELIZABETH. Farewell, thou woeful welcomer of glory.
ANNE. Adieu, poor soul, that tak'st thy leave of it.
DUCHESS. ... Go thou to Richard, and good angels guard thee—
Go thou to sanctuary, and good thoughts possess thee;
I to my grave, where peace and rest lie with me.

                                                        (4.1.32–95)

Phases	Secondary School Students	University Students
Noticing activity (Input)	• The teacher asks four students to read the lines of the characters in the scene. (S)he may help them by introducing the plot and main theme of *Richard III* (the Cambridge School Shakespeare series can be useful at this stage; see Brady and Coles, 2018).	• Students read the text by themselves and reflect on the role of the three female characters who act in the passage selected. Once they are familiar with the play, they may also read Lull's introduction to The New Cambridge Shakespeare edition of *King Richard III* (2009: 1–51) as an assignment.
	• A brainstorming activity will follow where students are invited to guess the communicative context of the passage selected, and the feelings expressed by each character, thus introducing the pragmatic dimension of speech acts inductively.	• Students are introduced to the field of historical pragmatics and diachronic speech act theory.
	• The teacher sums up the results by explaining Searle's (+ Leech's) speech act theory.	
Awareness activity (Scaffolding I)	Students will identify the speech acts in the passage selected, classify them according to Searle's (+ Leech's) taxonomy, and detect the grammar classes that introduce them (e.g., this commissive speech act is introduced by the imperative).	Students will identify the speech acts in the passage selected and classify them according to Austin's and Searle's (+ Leech's) taxonomies. They will then try to fit them into Jucker and Taavitsainen's framework of pragmatic space.

| Guided practice (Scaffolding II) | Rewrite the conversation downing the register (making it more colloquial) and modernising the language, even referring to the footnotes of the Cambridge edition or to pre-existing intralingual translations of the text (e.g., Shmoop or Sparknotes). Remember that the same speech acts of the original Shakespearean text must be maintained. | Write short sentences/paragraphs/memos (fifty words max) about the linguistic representation of women in the early modern period in England. The lecturer can provide students with an essential bibliography. |
| Autonomous practice (Output) | Students work in small groups (cooperative learning) and enact a role play whose protagonists are Anne, Elizabeth, and the Duchess of York. Elizabeth and the Duchess are two TV talk show presenters interviewing the future queen Anne who has just heard the news of her imminent coronation. Use as many kinds of speech acts as possible, following the theoretical framework presented during the noticing activity phase. | Students work in small groups (cooperative learning and peer tutoring) and prepare a presentation about the pragmalinguistic representation of female feelings and emotions in *Richard III*, stressing the pivotal role of expressive performative speech acts. Results will be shared with the other groups and discussed. |

Secondary School

After reading the text, secondary school students will take part in a collective brainstorming activity on the blackboard or smart board (using online resources such as MindMup, Miro, or Canva; see Figure 4). Students will guess the three characters' feelings when Stanley tells them that Anne is about to be Richard's wife.

Figure 4 An example of a secondary school brainstorming activity realised with MindMup.

The teacher then summarises the results of the brainstorming activity and focuses on how feelings are expressed by the three women, thus explaining what speech acts are and how they are conveyed linguistically (slides or flashcards can be used as supports).

University

University students attending a History of the English Language or Historical Linguistics course will be introduced to the field of historical pragmatics and diachronic speech act theory. This part of the module can be introduced as a traditional classroom-taught lesson or as a flipped classroom by dividing students into different groups and letting them prepare mini-lectures (15–20 minutes approximately) by referring to the bibliography used in the previous subsections.

Awareness Activity (Scaffolding I)

Secondary School

Using the taxonomy of speech acts identified by the teacher during the noticing activity phase, secondary school students will identify the speech acts in the passage selected and classify them according to Searle's and Leech's taxonomy (assertives, commissives, declarations, directives, expressives, rogatives). In addition, grammar and lexical elements which introduce and characterise each speech act will be identified in order to distinguish between explicit and implicit performatives; for example, 'Come, madam, you must straight to Westminster' (4.1.32) is a directive speech act pointed out by the imperative, but not by any performative verbs such as *order*, *command*, and so on; hence, it is an implicit directive. Results can be presented in a tabular form, as in Table 4.

University

University students will work with the different taxonomies of diachronic speech acts in more detail. They will identify speech acts in the scene selected and then try to classify them according to (1) Austin's, (2) Searle's and Leech's, and (3) Jucker and Taavitsainen's (adapted) frameworks, as in Table 5.

Guided Practice (Scaffolding II)

Secondary School

During this phase, secondary school students will rewrite the scene selected by referring to online dictionaries (Cambridge, Merriam-Webster, etc.), footnotes in the New Cambridge edition of *Richard III*, or modernised/ simplified versions available online (e.g., Shmoop, Sparknotes, etc.). They must also be careful to respect the classification elaborated during the

Table 4 An example of the classification of speech acts in the scene analysed.

Utterance	Kind of speech act	Grammar/lexical element characterising it	Explicit (also indicate the performative verb)	Implicit
Come, madam, you must straight to Westminster	Directive	Imperative		X
. . .				

Table 5 Classification of speech acts according to the different frameworks presented in Section 1.

| | Kind of speech act according to . . . taxonomy | | |
Utterance	Austin's	Searle's and Leech's	Jucker and Taavitsainen's[23]
I envy not thy glory	?	?	Formal level: ? Semantics: ? Context dependence: ? Speaker attitude: ? Reaction: ?
. . .			

awareness activity phase, thus maintaining the pragmatic and communicative intent of each speech act. For example, the expressives 'Poor heart, adieu; I pity thy complaining' (4.1.88) – greeting + explicit expressive introduced by the verb 'to pity' – can become 'Farewell, poor girl. I feel compassion for your complaint', still maintaining the pragmatic force of the two expressives included in Elizabeth's line.

University

University students, on the other hand, will write short sentences, paragraphs, or memos about the linguistic representation of female characters in early modern England, with a particular focus on the way they express feelings. Examples of short sentences or paragraphs can be as follows: 'In the passage from *Richard III*, 4.1, it is evident that female characters express their feelings explicitly and with no half measure', or 'Stanley's directive speech act underlines the patriarchal force of Richard's order. Although he is the Earl of Derby, and thus should be inferior to the Queen

---

[23] It is worth recalling that Jucker and Taavitsainen's framework of pragmatic space was initially created for other kinds of expressives, i.e., insults; hence, their taxonomy can be adapted here by changing/eliminating some of the categories or dimensions identified.

consort, he orders her to go to Westminster because the King himself has decreed it'. All written tasks can be collected and shared via online tools such as Padlet or Linoit (see Figure 5).

Autonomous Practice (Output)

Secondary School

In the optics of a creative output where spoken interactional skills are enhanced, secondary school students are given a talk show scenario where Elizabeth and the Duchess are the TV presenters who ask questions and react to Anne's answers. Anne has recently been engaged to Richard and is about to be crowned queen, and this is the first exclusive interview the soon-to-be queen grants to national television. As TV presenters, Elizabeth and the Duchess can have prompts and sticky notes to ask questions. At this stage, students must be capable of using as many kinds of speech acts as possible. Here is a sample conversation:

ELIZABETH: Ladies and gentlemen, direct from the Royal Palace, let's welcome our future queen consort, Miss Anne Neville! (Directive)

ANNE: Hello! Hello everybody! (Expressive)

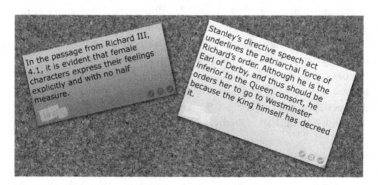

In the passage from Richard III, 4.1, it is evident that female characters express their feelings explicitly and with no half measure.

Stanley's directive speech act underlines the patriarchal force of Richard's order. Although he is the Earl of Derby, and thus should be inferior to the Queen consort, he orders her to go to Westminster because the King himself has decreed it.

Figure 5 Example of a guided practice task done with Linoit.

DUCHESS: So . . . how are you feeling today, Anne? (Rogative)
ANNE: [*Showing her enormous ring*] Well . . . engaged, maybe?!
             (Declaration)
ELIZABETH: Wow! [*Laughing*] Need any help carrying that?
             (Commissive)
ANNE: [*Laughing*] Actually, I think I'm OK! (Assertive)

             . . .

University

On the other hand, university students will work in small groups and prepare seminar-like presentations, with the support of slides or notes written down during the guided practice phase, about the pragmalinguistic strategies that female characters employ in *Richard III* to express their feelings and react to the patriarchal society they lived in. Additional bibliographical research is encouraged in order to widen the focus of the presentation and consider the entire history play and Shakespeare's works in general.

2 Teaching Shakespearean Discourse Markers with *Romeo and Juliet*

What are Discourse Markers?

Most scholars agree that defining *DMs* is almost impossible, since they 'are multifunctional linguistic expressions and [. . .] do not form a recognized (closed) word class' (Degand et al., 2013: 5). In Diana M. Lewis's terms, there is

> 'little consensus on whether they are a syntactic or a pragmatic category, on which types of expressions the category includes, on the relationship of discourse markers to other posited categories such as connectives, interjections, modal particles, speaker-oriented sentence adverbials, and on the term 'discourse marker' as opposed to alternatives such as

'discourse connective' or 'pragmatic marker' or 'pragmatic particle'. (2011: 419–20)[24]

Well aware of these theoretical and methodological issues, Chiara Fedriani and Andrea Sansò (2017: 2) propose a distinction between *pragmatic markers* (hereafter *PMs*), DMs, and *modal particles* (hereafter *MPs*), partially based on Chiara Ghezzi (2014):

> We intend PMs as markers of functions belonging to the domains of social and interpersonal cohesion (the hearer-speaker relationship, the social identity of H and S, the type of social act performed; e.g., please, danke, if I may interrupt, etc.) and DMs as strategies ensuring textual cohesion (discourse planning, discourse managing; e.g., utterance initial usages of but, anyway, still, etc.). The term MP, on the other hand, has a longer and better-established tradition, indicating a closed class of items that participate in a paradigm as signals of the speaker's evaluation of the information status of his/her utterance.

Nevertheless, in the same volume, Ludivine Crible (2017) affirms that the label 'discourse markers' should be preferred to 'pragmatic markers', the former indicating a broader class of elements governing and guiding conversation, a hypernymic category, an umbrella term which also includes PMs (Hansen, 2006: 28). For the purposes of this Element, I adopt Crible's viewpoint and deal with a general, pragmatic-oriented connotation of DMs as items that 'guide the hearer toward a particular interpretation of the connection between a sequence of utterances and at the same time rule out unintended interpretations' (Furkó, 2018: 158).

---

[24] Although scholars tend to distinguish between discourse markers, modal particles, pragmatic markers, and other labels, for the purposes of this study, I will not delve into rigid categorisations, focusing exclusively on the pragmatic dimension of DMs (see, for instance, Fedriani and Sansò, 2017: 3–8).

According to Jucker and Yael Ziv (1998: 3, adapted from Brinton, 1996: 33–35), DMs have the following basic characteristics (qtd. in Lutzky, 2012: 12):

- Phonological and lexical features:

  a. They are short and phonologically reduced.
  b. They form a separate tone group.
  c. They are marginal forms and hence difficult to place within a traditional word class.

- Syntactic features:

  d. They are restricted to sentence-initial position.
  e. They occur outside the syntactic structure, or they are only loosely attached to it.
  f. They are optional.

- Semantic feature:

  g. They have little or no propositional meaning.

- Functional feature:

  h. They are multifunctional, operating on several linguistic levels simultaneously.

- Sociolinguistic and stylistic features:

  i. They are a feature of oral rather than written discourse and are associated with informality.
  j. They appear with high frequency.
  k. They are stylistically stigmatised.
  l. They are gender-specific and more typical of women's speech.

Péter Furkó (2014, 2018) clearly summarises the main characteristics of DMs, referring to previous studies. According to his framework, DMs are:

1. Truth-conditional (propositional) or non-truth-conditional (non-propositional), that is, does a DM express a content or not? This distinction has been replaced by Diane Blakemore's relevance theory and

her division between conceptual and procedural meaning of DMs (1987; 2002, plus related criticism: see, e.g., Fraser, 2006; Wilson, 2016). Typically, DMs are procedural words that do not encode any concept, but help the Hs in their inferential procedures to understand the meaning of the Ss' utterances.

2. Syntactically and semantically optional, that is, if removed, the grammaticality and semantic meaning of the sentence they are inserted in are not altered (Schourup, 1999: 231). As stated by Brinton (1996: 1), DMs are 'grammatically optional and semantically or functionally unmotivated'.

3. Context-dependent: This property is directly connected to the indexicality of DMs, that is, their capability of indicating (indexing) an object in the context in which it occurs.

4. Multifunctional: 'DMs are also associated with a plethora of functions, including hedging and politeness functions. What is more, they can also be salient in conversational exchanges as openers, turn-taking devices, hesitation devices, backchannels, markers of topic shift and of receipt of information, and so on' (Furkó, 2018: 158).

5. Weakly associated with clauses: According to Crible (2017), DMs are not or only loosely part of the syntactic structure of a sentence.

6. Phonologically independent: DMs do not contribute to the general intonation of a sentence; yet they have their own 'comma intonation', that is, they are pronounced as if they were parenthetical or nonessential by pausing or changing the pitch before and/or after, according to their position within the sentence. Furkó (2014) asserts that this characteristic partially depends on the fact that historically DMs underwent a process of grammaticalisation and pragmaticalisation (see the next subsection), according to which some DMs originated from content, lexical words (i.e., words with a full, proper semantic meaning) and then became function words (i.e., words with almost no semantic meaning that merely perform a grammatical function).

7. Variable in scope: They can affect single words or entire sentences (e.g., in the string 'You and I', *and* connects two pronouns, while in the sentence 'You like coffee and I prefer tea', *and* links two clauses).

8. Highly frequent in speech: This forms the basis of the grammatica-lisation of DMs, according to Furkó (2014).
9. Mostly used in spoken interaction (see, for instance, Beeching, 2016).
10. Stigmatised by prescriptivists (Brown and Yule, 1983: 17), that is, they are associated with markers of lower registers, something to be (over) used in speech, but to be avoided when writing.

Before offering some useful taxonomies to categorise DMs, it is worth understanding why such 'insignificant words and innocuous particles' (Brinton, 1990: 45) should be considered by linguists. According to Brinton, DMs have various discursive functions (1990: 47–48):

- to initiate discourse
- to mark a boundary in discourse; that is, to indicate a shift or partial shift in topic
- to preface a response or a reaction
- to serve as a filler or delaying tactic
- to aid the speaker in holding the floor
- to effect an interaction or sharing between the speaker and the hearer
- to bracket the discourse either cataphorically or anaphorically
- to mark either foregrounded or backgrounded information.

Lutzky elaborates a similar, yet more complete, list of functions of DMs, distinguishing between structural and interactional functions, which is worth quoting here (see Table 6):

As stated in recent studies about DMs, Yael Maschler and Deborah Schiffrin's definition and categorisation (2015) seems to be an excellent 'up-to-date summarization' (Fedriani and Sansò, 2017: 1) of the issues surrounding DMs. According to Maschler and Schiffrin, there are three different perspectives on DMs 'in terms of their basic starting point, their definition of discourse markers, and their method of analysis' (2015: 190).

The first perspective derives from Schiffrin's sociolinguistic analysis, conducted through both quantitative and qualitative methods (1987), and underlines the close connection between markers and discourse, understood as 'a process of social interaction' (2015: 190).

Table 6 Potential discourse marker functions according to Ursula Lutzky, 2012: 39.

Structural	Interactional
• Initiating function	• Conveying positive or negative attitudes
• Closing or conclusive function	• Attention-catching
• Turn-taking devices	• Hesitation devices, fillers
• Frame function, marking boundaries in discourse (e.g., topic changes/shifts, digressions, etc.)	• Face-threat mitigation (hedging)
	• Acknowledging function
	• Qualifier function (signalling some kind of insufficiency)
• Quotative function	• Intensifying function
• Introducing parts of an adjacency pair	

This analysis led to the definition of DMs as 'non-obligatory utterance-initial items that function in relation to ongoing talk and text' (2015: 191). As for grammar class, DMs belong to (1) conjunctions, (2) interjections, (3) adverbs, and (4) lexicalised phrases, such as '*y'know, I mean*' (191, Emphasis in the original).

The second approach, by Bruce Fraser (1998, 2009a, 2009b), is pragmatic and considers 'how one type of pragmatic marker in a sentence may relate the message conveyed by that sentence to the message of a prior sentence' (Maschler and Schiffrin, 2015: 192–93). In other words, Fraser's broader framework analyses the relationship between two sentences – or discourse segment, according to Fraser's definition (2009a: 296) – connected by a PM. Fraser's framework distinguishes between four types of PMs (qtd. in Maschler and Schiffrin, 2015: 193):

1. Basic PMs (signals of illocutionary force, e.g., *please*)
2. Commentary PMs (encoding of another message that comments on the basic message, e.g., *frankly*)

3. Parallel PMs (encoding of another message separate from the basic and/ or commentary message, e.g., *damn*, vocatives)
4. Discourse management markers 'which signal a metacomment on the structure of the discourse' (Fraser, 2009b: 893).

DMs are included in the second category as commentary PMs, which is 'a class of expressions, each of which signals how the speaker intends the basic message that follows to relate to the prior discourse' (Fraser, 1998: 387). Discourse markers are categorised into three functional classes (Fraser, 2009a: 300–01):

1. Contrastive (e.g., *but*)
2. Elaborative (e.g., *and*)
3. Inferential (e.g., *so*).

Lastly, Maschler's interactionist approach (1994 and following) focuses on the text and the function(s) of a DM within a given context. According to his framework (1998; Maschler and Schiffrin, 2015: 194–98), DMs belong to 'four realms of discourse' (Maschler, 1998: 13):

1. Textual–referential: deictics and conjunctions.
2. Textual–structural: They mark order or hierarchy within the discourse (e.g., *first of all*). Both kinds of textual DMs connect 'prior and upcoming discourse' (Maschler and Schiffrin, 2015: 196).
3. Interpersonal–interactional, which account for the relations between S and H (epistemic DMs, modal DMs).[25]
4. Cognitive, which show the development of the S's cognitive processes during conversation (e.g., *Oh, I see*, to express that new information is being processed).

---

[25] Epistemic DMs refer to the distribution of knowledge between S and H. For example, in the dialogue 'A: Are you coming to Sheila's party tomorrow? B: *But* Bob invited us for a drink for his birthday', the conjunction *but*, instead of fulfilling its traditional adversative function, indicates that B thinks A should already have some knowledge of the content of what (s)he is uttering. Modal DMs 'express meanings associated with the relationship between' S and H (Romano and Cuenca, 2013: 348).

DMs in Early Modern English

The first studies that focused on diachronic perspectives on DMs (see, e.g., Stein, 1985; Brinton, 1990) observed how difficult it was to cope with such a thorny category, which was 'linguistically ephemeral' (Stein, 1985: 300) and 'transitory in nature' (Brinton, 1990: 49). On the one hand, DMs are difficult to define; on the other hand, diachronic perspectives make things much more complicated. In this subsection, some questions concerning the diachronic development and study of DMs will be considered.

When adopting a historical perspective to deal with DMs, it is worth considering some processes that characterised this linguistic category. First of all, as highlighted by the frameworks presented in the previous paragraph (esp. Brown and Yule, 1983: 17; Brinton, 1996: 33–35; Jucker and Ziv, 1998: 3), DMs are highly stigmatised since their presence in written texts is often associated with lower stylistic registers, as they are typical of oral language and spoken interaction. As noted by Brinton (1990: 46), they are 'stylistically deplored'. This was particularly true in the history of the English language, when DMs 'were regarded as mere fillers [and] they were often negatively evaluated when occurring in OE [Old English] and ME [Middle English] texts' (Lutzky, 2012: 25). While pronunciation, grammar, and vocabulary have received much attention from English historical linguists, communication and spoken interaction has not. As noted by Jucker (2002: 210), 'research into the history of English has tended to focus on pronunciation, the structure of words and the structure of sentences, but not on the communicative aspects of the language and on the interaction between speakers of the language'.

Nevertheless, as observed in the previous sections, theatrical texts represent a privileged field of study to be considered, given their speech-purposed nature, something that position them between written and oral language. According to Brinton (1990), a plethora of scholars have argued the oral nature of theatrical texts such as early modern plays: the written text was often a mere plot outline for actors who usually changed and adapted it before uttering their lines before the audience. In this sense, DMs cannot be considered stigmatised items, but markers of the speech-purposed nature of early modern plays, what Brinton calls 'stylized discourse markers' (1990: 59), elements that signal 'oral feature[s] . . . in written discourse' (59).

Another paramount issue to consider in studying DMs from a historical point of view is the process that led some words to lose their semantic fullness and become DMs, that is, grammaticalisation, or, in most cases discussed here, pragmaticalisation. Sandra A. Thompson and Anthony Mulac (1991) state that some DMs derive from lexical items which acquired a mere grammatical value. For example, *I mean* and *You know* lost their primary semantic meaning – this process is known as semantic bleaching – to carry out a grammatical function, although Karin Aijmer (1997) prefers calling this process pragmaticalisation or pragmatic strengthening, whereby 'a lexicalised structure is recruited to serve a pragmatic function that involves the speaker's attitude towards the hearer' (Jucker, 2002: 216). To understand the difference between grammaticalisation and pragmaticalisation, Aijmer uses the example of *to be going to*, where four lexical items combined together began to express the grammatical function of futurity. Conversely, such expressions as *I mean* or *You know* underwent a process of pragmatic strengthening, serving pragmatic instead of grammatical functions.

But how did scholars analyse DMs in the early modern period (in drama especially) and which DMs did they consider? Referring to the Helsinki Corpus, a repository of almost 450 texts from different genres, ranging from 730 to 1710 CE, Jucker analyses the distribution of the five most recurring DMs in the corpus – that is, *o/oh, why, well, pray/prithee, marry* – focusing on early modern plays, the written genre which contains the highest percentage of occurrences of DMs in the whole corpus – that is, 9.2 hits per 1,000 words – for the reasons discussed in the previous paragraphs. As Jucker explains,

> *Oh* is a discourse marker that could also be analysed as an interjection. The discourse marker *why*, on the other hand, must be distinguished from the question particle or conjunction *why*. *Well* is the most prototypical discourse marker. ... *Pray* and *prithee* are pragmaticalised forms of the parenthetical phrase *I pray you/thee* and serve as markers of deference. *Marry*, finally, is a pragmaticalised form of the religious invocation *by the Virgin Mary*. *Oh* and *well* still exist in Present Day English, *why* is restricted to

> American English, and *pray/prithee* and *marry* are only
> used as archaisms or humorously – if at all – in Present
> Day English. (Jucker, 2002: 229)

The conclusions reached are articulated in three fundamental points:

> First, the distribution of discourse markers is genre specific
> and linked to orality. In Early Modern English they are
> more or less restricted to the genres play, fiction and trial
> records. ... Second, the frequency of discourse markers
> varies in time. Some markers increase in popularity and
> become more frequent, while other markers drop out of
> use and become obsolete. ... And finally, several of the
> discourse markers analysed above could be shown to be the
> result of a pragmaticalisation process. (229–30)

Lutzky devotes an entire monograph to DMs in Early Modern English
(2012), analysing both quantitatively and qualitatively the occurrences of
marry, *well*, and *why* in four historical corpora – that is, the Corpus of
English Dialogues 1560–1760, the Parsed Corpus of Early English
Correspondence, the Penn-Helsinki Parsed Corpus of Early Modern
English, and the Drama Corpus – and carries out a sociopragmatic
analysis of the results obtained. Unlike Jucker, who focused on
a restricted sample of genres, Lutzky analyses 'a range of authentic and
fictional text types, which either record spoken EModE (trial proceedings,
witness depositions) or imitate it (drama comedy, prose fiction, didactic
works), which were written to be spoken (sermon) or which may be
regarded as speech-related due to their interactive and involved nature
(letter, diary)' (2012: 266). Lutzky's conclusions are important and shed
some light on the use of DMs by Early Modern English playwrights such
as Shakespeare:

> All of them [i.e., *marry*, *well*, and *why*] cluster in dialogic and
> fictional texts which have been said to imitate spoken lan-
> guage. On the other hand, they are less frequent in authentic

and in monologic texts. Consequently, one may conclude that discourse markers are indeed prominent interactional features and that even during the EModE period authors may have been aware of their particularly speech-like nature and hence included them specifically when constructing speech. Furthermore, this study could uncover sociopragmatic tendencies, with particular markers being attested primarily in the talk of characters of a particular social status or gender; this implies that playwrights may have used them intentionally for purposes of characterisation. (270)

Therefore, what is important to underline for the purposes of this volume is that even in the early modern period, DMs were used more in speech-purposed or related text types, and that playwrights might have used them to characterise certain characters with a particular social status or gender, as the next subsections will show.

DMs in Romeo and Juliet

Studies about DMs in Shakespeare's *Romeo and Juliet* are scant and often part of broader linguistic investigations of the play's peculiar language.[26] Culpeper (2009, 2014), for instance, analyses words, parts of speech, and semantic categories in *Romeo and Juliet* using corpus linguistics, and among the different linguistic items he considers there are also DMs. By exploring the most recurrent keywords for each character, Culpeper concludes that DMs are 'clearly established as a feature of the Nurse's speech' (2009: 45, 2014: 48), thus confirming Lutzky's hypothesis that DMs are typical not only of speech-purposed texts, but also of 'characters of a particular social status or gender' (2012: 270), in this case women of the lower classes. Culpeper lists the most recurring DMs uttered by the nurse. Such words as *o* (16 hits), *ah* (6), *ay* (5), *nay* (4),

---

[26] It is important to note that there are three distinct versions of *Romeo and Juliet*: Q1 (the quarto of 1597), Q2 (the quarto of 1599), and F (the Folio text of 1623). Most of the studies presented here focus on analysing Q2 or on a collation of the three versions.

alas (3), *no* (2), *amen* (1), *ho* (1), *yes* (1), *fie* (1), and *farewell* (1) were not part of the keywords found by the software and it is worth noting this aspect now, because it provides important information about the uniqueness of the nurse's linguistic choices, in addition to highlighting the limitations of the part of speech (PoS) tagging, which was exactly one of Culpeper's aims – something that is not important to our study. Moreover, Culpeper's findings shed important light on the lexical items used as DMs by Shakespeare, some of which we find obsolete nowadays and need to be modernised or carefully explained when introduced to students (especially secondary school students). Such words as *alas* or *fie*, for example, might be translated intralingually with the aid of the Cambridge Dictionary online, or recurring to modernised/simplified versions of *Romeo and Juliet* (e.g., the Cambridge School Shakespeare, edited by Smith, 2014). One may argue that obsolete, archaic DMs can be omitted when focusing on the linguistic aspects of *Romeo and Juliet* that are worth being taught in ESL classes, since they are not strictly necessary to an understanding of the semantic meaning of a sentence. Nevertheless, I agree with Farahani and Ghane (2022) that DMs 'play a pivotal role in pragmatic competence of speakers ... and will help them to make their speech more comprehensible and rich ... as well as more sociable' (49).

Drawing on Brinton's categorisation and description of DMs in Early Modern English (2010: 290–92), Busse and Busse (2012) elaborate a taxonomy of DMs in Shakespeare's canon that is worth recording:

1. One-word DMs: *Anon, marry, only, right, videlicet, what, why* 1.a. Interjections: *ah, alas, fie, oh, tush, welaway*

2. Phrasal DMs/markers of phrasal origin: *Actually, anyway, as far as, besides, indeed, in fact, it / that is to wit > to wit*

3. Parentheticals of clausal origin: *God forbid, I'm sorry, (I) pray (thee/you) / prithee, I promise, I thank you / I give thanks to you > thank you / thanks*

4. Comment clauses: *(as) I gather, (as) you say, hark (you / ye) > harkee / harkey, I expect, if you will, I mean, (I) say, look (you / ye) > lookee / lookey, what's else, what's more.*

This taxonomy will be adopted in the following subsection to help secondary school and university students deal with the complex panorama of DMs in *Romeo and Juliet*.

Another model that will be adopted in the lesson plan about *Romeo and Juliet* is by David and Ben Crystal (2002).[27] Unlike Brinton's framework, which is clearly based on syntactic patterns, Crystal and Crystal elaborated their own taxonomy based on the positioning of S and H and on the communicative intention of the sentence(s) uttered, which can be accessed online at the URL www.shakespeareswords.com/Public/LanguageCompanion/ThemesAnd Topics.aspx?TopicId=11. The Crystals' framework is furnished with examples from the Shakespearean canon and the modernised version of the early modern DMs. Categories and examples of DMs from Shakespeare's plays are provided as follows:

- S draws H's attention to a point: *o' conscience*; *I fear me*; *good deed*; *good now*; *know't*; *la*; *la you*; *law*; *look you*; *I prithee*; *I protest*; *say*; *think it*
- S reformulates or adds to a point: *Nay, more*; *which is more*
- S summarizes a point: *This is for all*, *be it concluded*; *in few*; *once this*; *at a word*; *within a word*
- S lets H know the utterance is about to end: *There is an end*; *even so much*; *in fine*; *soft*
- S lets H know the topic is changing: *What though*
- An alternative or contrast: *Nay*; *but nay*
- A stronger degree of affirmation or assurance than 'yes': *E'en so*; *with all my heart*; *I warrant you*; *what else?*
- A stronger degree of denial or rejection than 'no': *Let go*
- A confirmation check on what S has just said: *Pray ye?*; *Say you?*; *Say'st me so?*
- A prompt for S to continue: *Good*; *make that good*; *have you at*; *trow*
- An acknowledgement that S has made a point: *Go to*; *you have said*

---

[27] As explained in the website, *Shakespeare's Words* was published in 2002 as both a (Penguin) book and a website. Since then, the website has been enriched periodically (up to 2022 by now), including the list of DMs presented in this Element. Hence, I choose to introduce this study at this point, following the discussion on Brinton (2010).

- An acknowledgment of S's attitude: *Come*; *you may*
- An expression of unwillingness to continue with S's topic: *That's/'tis all one*; *I have said*; *go thy ways*
- An expression of response uncertainty to S: *O Lord, sir*
- Elicit action, not further speech: *Come your ways*; *have with you.*

Lesson Plan 2

Noticing Activity (Input)

Secondary School

During the input phase, all students familiarise themselves with the lines selected from the Shakespearean text (2.4.121–81). The teacher may introduce *Romeo and Juliet*'s plot and main themes to secondary school students, while university students should know the play in advance by reading it and/or Blakemore Evans' introduction to The New Cambridge Shakespeare edition (2018: 1–62).

Since secondary school students are provided with a gapped text with no DMs, they will undergo a multiple-choice listening comprehension where the suitable DM must be chosen among a list of three items, as in the following example:

NURSE: _____, sir, what saucy merchant was this, that was so full of his ropery?

a) Prithee
b) I pray you
c) I promise you

Audiobooks of *Romeo and Juliet* can be used (e.g., www.youtube.com/watch?v=e4tSfkGyC74) or short video clips from key productions, such as Erica Whyman's 2018 production for the Royal Shakespeare Company (RSC). The teacher then checks the answers of the activity and focuses on the DMs' frameworks – especially Brinton (2010) and Crystal and Crystal (2002). Slides and/or flashcards may be used as support.

NURSE. *[Referring to Mercutio who has just left the stage]* Marry, farewell! I pray you, sir, what saucy merchant was this, that was so full of his ropery?

ROMEO. A gentleman, Nurse, that loves to hear himself talk . . .

NURSE. And 'a speak any thing against me, I'll take him down . . . And thou must stand by too, and suffer every knave to use me at his pleasure!

PETER. I saw no man use you at his pleasure; if I had, my weapon should quickly have been out. I warrant you. . . .

NURSE. Now, afore God, I am so vexed, that every part about me quivers. Scurvy knave! Pray you, sir, a word: and as I told you, my young lady bade me inquire you out; what she bade me say, I will keep to myself: but first let me tell ye, if ye should lead her into a fool's paradise, as they say, it were a very gross kind of behavior, as they say: for the gentlewoman is young; and, therefore, if you should deal double with her, truly it were an ill thing to be offered to any gentlewoman, and very weak dealing.

. . . ROMEO. Bid her devise

Some means to come to shrift this afternoon,

And there she shall at Friar Lawrence' cell

Be shrived and married. Here is for thy pains.

. . . NURSE. This afternoon, sir? well, she shall be there. . . . Now God in heaven bless thee! Hark you, sir. . . . My mistress is the sweetest lady – Lord, Lord! when 'twas a little prating thing:– O, there is a nobleman in town, one Paris, that would fain lay knife aboard; but she, good soul, had as lieve see a toad, a very toad, as see him. I anger her sometimes and tell her that Paris is the properer man, but I'll warrant you, when I say so, she looks as pale as any clout in the versal world. Doth not rosemary and Romeo begin both with a letter?

ROMEO. Ay, Nurse, what of that? both with an R.

NURSE. Ah. mocker! that's the dog-name. R is for the – no, I know it begins with some other letter – and she hath the prettiest sententious of it, of you and rosemary, that it would do you good to hear it.

ROMEO. Commend me to thy lady.

NURSE. Ay, a thousand times.

[Exit Romeo]

Peter!

PETER. Anon.

NURSE. *[Handing him her fan.]* Before and apace.

Exeunt

(2.4.121−81)[28]

Phases	Secondary School Students	University Students
Noticing activity (Input)	• A gapped version of the text selected is provided. The teacher asks three students to read the lines of the characters in the scene and the rest of the class is invited to fill the gaps by guessing the missing DM. The teacher may help them by introducing the plot and main theme of *Romeo and Juliet* (the Cambridge School Shakespeare book series can be useful at this stage; see Smith, 2014). • A listening comprehension will follow in the form of a multiple-choice quiz (see next paragraph for details) where students are invited to choose the correct DM from a list of three items. In this manner, they can confirm the accuracy of their earlier responses.	• Students read the text by themselves and guess the grammatical, semantic, and pragmatic value of the DMs highlighted by the lecturer. Once they are familiar with the play, they can also read Gwynne Blakemore Evans' introduction to The New Cambridge Shakespeare edition of *Romeo and Juliet* (2018: 1−62) as an assignment. • Students are introduced to the field of historical DMs and the various frameworks to classify them. Special attention should be paid to gender issues (Lutzky, 2012: 270, 2016).

[28] All quotations from *Romeo and Juliet* are taken from the New Cambridge edition, edited by G. Blakemore Evans. Only act, scene, and line numbers will be quoted in the main text. See references for more details. As this edition relies on the Q2 text of the play and collations with Q1 and F, I will exclusively examine speech acts as they appear in the 1623 version.

	• Results are checked and DMs are introduced, with particular attention to Brinton's 2010 and Crystal and Crystal's 2002 taxonomies.	
Awareness activity (Scaffolding I)	Referring to Crystal and Crystal's glosses (2002), students will work on the modernisation of the DMs identified in the previous exercise. The teacher can help them understand which DMs are obsolete – and thus need to be modernised – and which are still used in contemporary English.	Drawing mainly on Brinton (2010) and Crystal and Crystal (2002), students will classify DMs in the passage selected, providing justification(s) for their choices as well as a detailed description of the communicative context each DM can be inserted in.
Guided practice Scaffolding II)	A written exercise is given, where some statements are provided, and students are asked to react to them using the most appropriate DM(s).	In preparation of the autonomous practice phase, students are given pieces of formal and informal letters to be recognised and classified. Stylistic implications of the use of DMs should be highlighted (Kapranov, 2018) and an exercise on the change of register is provided.
Autonomous practice (Output)	Students work in groups of three (cooperative learning). They are required to create a WhatsApp group whose components are the Nurse, Romeo, and Peter, with the aim of arranging Romeo and Juliet's marriage. The use of DMs should be elicited.	Students are asked to write a(n) (in)formal letter to another character in *Romeo and Juliet*, inviting her/him to the wedding. Discourse markers should be used in order to set the tone and register of the letter.

University

University students should know the play in advance by reading it and studying Blakemore Evans' introduction to The New Cambridge Shakespeare edition (2018: 1–62). They will be introduced to the field of historical DMs. This part of the module can be introduced as a traditional classroom-taught lesson or as a flipped classroom by dividing students into different groups and letting them prepare mini-lectures (15–20 minutes approximately) by referring to the bibliography used in the previous subsections. Given the scholarly debate surrounding the inherent sociolinguistic aspects of DMs (e.g., the gender and social class of the speaker, as highlighted by Lutzky, 2012: 270, 2016), particular attention will be devoted to these features.

Awareness Activity (Scaffolding I)

Secondary School

During this phase, secondary school pupils will mainly use Crystal and Crystal's taxonomy of DMs (2002) and their glosses to classify and modernise the DMs they have already identified in the previous exercise. The teacher will function as a monitor and help students understand which DMs are perceived as obsolete in contemporary English and need to be modernised. An example of an exercise is provided as follows (see Table 7):

University

Similarly, university students will integrate Brinton's (2010) and Crystal and Crystal's (2002) framework, thus classifying DMs in the passage from *Romeo and Juliet*. They will provide justification(s) for their choices as well as a detailed description of the communicative context in which each DM is inserted in the play, as in the following example (see Table 8):

Table 7 Example of an exercise about the identification and modernisation of DMs in *Romeo and Juliet*.

Line(s)	DM	Modernised version
NURSE: I pray you, sir, a word	I pray you	Excuse me, sir, a word / Can I have a word with you, sir?

Table 8 Example of an exercise about integrating Brinton's (2010) and Crystal and Crystal's (2002) taxonomies of Early Modern English DMs.

| Line(s) | DM | Classification according to | | Justification/ contextualisation |
		Brinton (2010)	Crystal and Crystal (2002)	
NURSE: I pray you, sir, a word	I pray you	Parenthetical of clausal origin	Within X's speech X draws Y's attention to a point	In such context, the Nurse is . . .

Guided Practice (Scaffolding II)

Secondary School

Since the output by both secondary school and university students will be in written form, the second part of the scaffolding will guide them to master written skills when DMs are involved. Secondary school students will be provided with some statements to which pupils are asked to react by using the most appropriate (modernised when necessary) DM(s), as in the following example:

A: My little kitty has just gone missing.
B: <u>Oh</u>, <u>I'm sorry</u>. How can I help you?

University

University students, on the other hand, will be given pieces of formal and informal real letters in Early Modern English to be recognised and classified. Stylistic implications of the use of DMs should be highlighted (Kapranov, 2018; Molinelli, 2018, p. 285), and an exercise on register switch will be provided in order to make students aware of the most suitable DMs for either formal or informal style.

Autonomous Practice (Output)

Secondary School

Secondary school students will work in groups of three in a cooperative learning environment. They will create a fake WhatsApp group whose components are the Nurse, Romeo, and Peter, with the aim of arranging Romeo and Juliet's marriage. The use of DMs should, of course, be elicited. Free websites such as fakewhats.com or fakedetail.com can be used (see Figure 6).

Figure 6 An example of secondary school students' output created using fakedetail.com.

University

On the other hand, considering the significance bestowed upon letters, or rather their failure to reach their intended recipients, in this Shakespearean tragedy, university students will be tasked with composing either formal or informal letters. The choice between formal and informal styles will depend on the gender and social class of both the sender and the recipient. The assignment will involve inviting another character in *Romeo and Juliet* to attend the wedding of the central couple. Discourse markers should be used in order to set the tone and register of the letter.

3 (Im)polite Shakespeare in *The Taming of the Shrew*

Teaching S-T Words in the EFL Classroom: 'Is [it] still a taboo?'[29]

Current literature in the field of English Language Teaching takes for granted that *swearwords and taboo expressions* (henceforth *S-T words*, as studies usually refer to them) are noteworthy socio-pragmatic phenomena that deserve attention by both teachers and students, without too much ado about ethical or moral implications traditionally associated with their role in educational environments (see, among others, Mercury, 1995; Horan, 2013; Kaduce and Metzger, 2019; Wedlock, 2020). For example, in her study on teaching English insults[30] with the aid of audiovisual material, Silvia Bruti (2016) simply considers S-T words as 'conversational routines', exactly as any other speech acts, 'conversational features' to be managed, since they are 'an essential instrument to interact in a foreign language' that 'is very often marginalized in syllabi' (153). Although this introduction to this final section of the Element may seem an unsolicited excuse, I would like to offer a brief overview of the importance and value of teaching S-T words in the EFL classroom.

First of all, I completely agree with Michael Adams' assertion that 'the more knowledgeable and therefore best educated on the subjects of "bad" words and language generally – will likely make the best decisions about their use' (2002: 357). In the 1990s, scholars such as Vivian de Klerk (1991) and Robin-Eliece Mercury (1995) had already highlighted the sociolinguistic and sociopragmatic importance of teaching and learning S-T words. De Klerk considered taboo language a revealing instrument to understand 'the social variables by which speakers are affected' (1991: 164), while Mercury encouraged ESL teachers and learners 'to consider [S-T words']

---

[29] This quotation is from an interesting article published in *The Guardian* (9 Februrary 2023) by Emine Saner, entitled 'OMG! Is Swearing Still a Taboo?'

[30] Insults can be considered a subgroup of S-T words. To avoid intrusive repetitions, I will use the labels *swearwords*, *taboo expressions/words*, *S-T words*, and *insults* interchangeably when and where possible.

sociolinguistic importance' (1995: 28). A decade later, Jean-Marc Dewaele advocated the implementation of taboo language in the ESL classroom as a means for pragmatic development (2007), while more recently Indika Liyanage et al. (2015) have examined teaching S-T words in terms of a language's authenticity. In short, when used appropriately, S-T terms can be considered an index of authenticity in ESL teaching. This could lead to considerations about the authenticity of the Shakespearean text as one of the most representative and original examples of Early Modern English interactional language, although such a thorny debate is beyond the scope of this Element. (However, see, among others, Busse and Busse, 2017.)

Joshua Wedlock considers Adams' approach a prevention-is-better-than-cure one and goes on to underline the lexico-pragmatic importance of teaching what he calls *SOTL* (*Swearing, Offensive, and Taboo Language*):

> I would argue that employing the same approach as espoused by Adams, but in the EFL/ESL classroom, would help equip EFL/ESL students with the appropriate knowledge required to understand the various forms and functions of SOTL, thus helping to ensure that English-language students don't make the types of lexical or pragmatic errors which could cause them (or others) undue embarrassment, stress, or other undesirable ramifications as a result of the misuse or abuse of SOTL. (2020: 34)

Teachers as well may offer interesting perspectives on the efficacy of teaching Shakespearean taboo words to their students. Sarah Swan, for instance, affirms that 'insulting' her students with the language of Shakespeare has humoristic effects in her English classrooms, allowing her to better capture the attention of her pupils (Swan, 2013). This is how she describes her approach: 'The theorist would frame this approach in terms of bridging the gap between high and low culture, but actually my thoughts were more practical. I just wanted to try and get them to understand the text, feel less intimidated by the 'poshness' of Shakespeare's language and Elizabethan sentence structure'.

The same approach had already been adopted by Cynthia J. Ottchen and Wayne F. Hill (1991, 1996), who published didactic booklets from both a student- and teacher-centred perspective to inform their intended readers about the many ways Shakespeare's characters insult each other. Students were invited to educate their wit (as the subtitle of their 1991 publication has it), while the teacher-oriented approach of their 1996 booklet aimed to create moments of comic relief and humour while teaching Shakespeare to both native and non-native students of English (exactly as in Swan's experience).

Similarly, the British Council tutor and resource writer Genevieve White proposed focusing on quick-fire dialogues full of insults and '[m]ake sure ... learners deliver their lines in as nasty a way as possible' (2015). At least this approach would allow teachers to make their students feel closer to Shakespeare, make his literary output more attractive to them, and bridge the gap between high and low culture, as Swan has stated.

And lest one think that teaching Shakespeare's S-T words should be reserved for adult learners only, there are scholars and instructors who actually disagree. Joe Winston and Miles Tandy (2012), for example, advise teachers to begin implementing insults in early childhood, with children aged four to eleven, because 'in Shakespeare's work, the colourful and tense language of insult and aggression is not directed at anyone in the classroom but at people in a fiction' (4). Addressing their book to primary school teachers, Stefan Kucharczyk and Maureen Kucharczyk (2022) agree with Winston and Tandy, asserting that insults 'are delicious to use and will become a staple of your drama lessons. They are also very useful for adding authenticity and spice to descriptive writing' (39). Here, once again, the question of authenticity arises when dealing with offensive language in Shakespeare.

The pro-SOTL teaching approach described here will be adopted in this last section of the Element, in the belief that ESL students must be aware of the pragmatic contexts of use of S-T words in order to avoid offending their interlocutors in certain contexts.

(Im)politeness Strategies in The Taming of the Shrew[31]

There is no doubt that, among Shakespeare's comedies, *The Taming of the Shrew* is one of the most interesting to analyse in terms of S-T words or SOTL (Dupuis and Tiffany, 2013). According to pragmaticians, taboo language belongs to the theory of impoliteness,[32] but even before late-twentieth-century linguistic studies about S-T words and impoliteness, insults and offences were considered threats to an addressee's self-image (or face)[33] by sociologists such as Ervin Goffman, who paved the way to face-based pragmatic models of (im)politeness and was the first to deal with

---

[31] I must here thank my dear friend a colleague Bianca Del Villano (University of Naples 'L'Orientale'), a fine scholar whose study, *Using the Devil with Courtesy. Shakespeare and the Language of (Im)politeness* (2018), inspired my career and forms the very core of this section of my Element (esp. pp. 138–71). I must also thank my (former) student – now a very good friend – Michaela Maturi from Sapienza University of Rome for her valuable assistance while I was writing this section of the Element. Her thesis, *"Nulla è bene e male in sé, ma è il pensiero chelo rende tale": Analisi linguistica di parolacce e insulti nel teatro shakespeariano* (*"There is nothing either good or bad, but thinking makes it so": Linguistic analysis of swearwords and insults in the Shakespearean theatre*), eloquently summarizes the considerations presented in the following subsections.

[32] Impoliteness as a theory was developed in response to Brown and Levinson's well-known face-based model of politeness (*Politeness: Some Universals in Language Use*, 1978/87) and following adjustments. For reasons of space and scope, their politeness framework is not dealt with in this Element.

[33] Goffman defines 'face' as the public self-image each S and H wants the others to see and approve/not to obstruct (1967: 5, emphasis in the original: 'The term *face* may be defined as the positive social value a persona effectively claims for himself .... Face is an image of self delineated in terms of approved social attributes').

SOTL by distinguishing between intentional and incidental, or unintentional, insults and offences (1967: 14). Referring to Goffman, pragmaticians 'seized upon intention as a means of identifying 'genuine' impoliteness' (Culpeper, 2021: 6), as Derek Bousfield's definition of impoliteness clearly states: 'Impoliteness constitutes the communication of intentionally gratuitous and conflictive verbal face-threatening acts which are purposefully delivered' (2008: 72).

In 1980, Lance Lachenicht was the first linguist to try to analyse interactions where the S intentionally wants to hurt the H's facework (i.e., the communicative strategies employed to maintain face or social prestige) by building a theoretical framework of impoliteness based on Brown and Levinson's well-known model of politeness. Lachenicht distinguishes four superstrategies of what he calls aggravating language: (1) indirect (off-record) aggravating language (i.e., ambiguous and ironic insults), (2) direct (bald on-record) aggravating language, (3) positive aggravating language (the H does not have the S's approval), and (4) negative aggravating language (the H receives an order by the S). Lachenicht's model, 'which presented problems with both the theory and methodology' (Bousfield and Culpeper, 2008: 161), was readjusted in 1990 by Paddy Austin, who proposed a six-phase H-based framework of impoliteness, and then by Culpeper in 1996. Culpeper's model[34] and its ensuing developments/integrations (esp. 2011a, 2011b, 2016, 2017, 2018, 2021) are the most widespread and authoritative today in the field of face-based impoliteness, even from a diachronic perspective, which is the one adopted in this Element. As a matter of fact, as Jucker and Taavitsainen note, '[i]nherently [(im)]polite speech acts can be more sensitive to changes of fashion and cultural variation (cf. the contrary meanings of gestures in different cultures), but, at the same time, this principle must hold at some level' (2008: 4).

---

[34] Even in this case, space considerations do not allow Culpeper's complex impoliteness framework to be outlined in this Element. However, readers may consult the Element's bibliographical references for further information about the topic.

Culpeper includes S-T words in what he calls *positive impoliteness output strategies*, 'the use of strategies designed to damage the addressee's positive face wants' (1996: 356), where positive face means 'the positive consistent self-image or 'personality' (crucially including the desire that this self-image be appreciated and approved of) claimed by interactants' (Brown and Levinson, 1978/87: 61), or, in other words, 'the want of every member that his wants be desirable to at least some others' (62). When an S wants to damage the H's self-image, positive impoliteness occurs and taboo words – 'swear, or use abusive or profane language' (Culpeper, 1996: 358) – are one of the possible strategies to employ.

In their sociocultural framework of taboo words, Allan and Burridge (2006) propose a slightly different model of S-T words, which however can be connected and integrated with Culpeper's taxonomy of impoliteness, since they 'examine politeness and impoliteness as they interact with orthophemism (straight talking), euphemism (sweet talking) and dysphemism (speaking offensively)' (1). It is clear that, in the case of this section of the Element, dysphemism is the category we must consider, as 'bald on-record' aggravating language (Lachenicht, 1980: 619) is now the object of research. Allan and Burridge's definition and examples of dysphemism are particularly useful here, since they are a good introduction to the world of SOTL in *The Taming of the Shrew* for readers, teachers, and learners:

> Dysphemisms are ... characteristic of political groups and cliques talking about their opponents; of feminists speaking about men; and also of male larrikins and macho types speaking of women and effete behaviours. Dysphemistic expressions include curses, name-calling, and any sort of derogatory comment directed towards others in order to insult or to wound them. Dysphemism is also a way to let off steam; for example, when exclamatory swear words alleviate frustration or anger. To be more technical: a dysphemism is a word or phrase with connotations that are offensive either about the denotatum and/ or to people addressed or overhearing the utterance. (2006: 31)

Table 9 Readaptation of Jucker and Taavitsainen's 'multidimensional space of … insults' (2000: 74, 2008: 6).

Levels	From …	… to
Formal level:	Ritual, rule governed	Creative
	Typified	Ah hoc
Semantics:	Truth-conditional	Performative
Context dependence:	Conventional	Particular
Speaker attitude:	Ludic	Aggressive
	Intentional	Unintentional
	Ironic	Sincere
Reaction:	Reaction in kind	Denial, violence, silence

Of course, what is considered an insult today may not have been considered offensive in Shakespeare's day. Moreover, 'What people considered insulting is a matter of culture to a large extent' (Jucker and Taavitsainen, 2008: 6). For this reason, Jucker and Taavitsainen elaborated a framework of the 'pragmatic space of insults' (2000: 74)[35] which could also take into account the diachronic variation of SOTL. See Table 2, or Table 9, which presents a graphically simplified version of the same:

As Jucker and Taavitsainen explain,

> The first two dimensions concern the formal level of the insults. There are two dimensions involved: the ritual as rule-governed versus the creative as not following conventionalized patterns, and the … typified and *ad hoc* insults. In some fictional genres insults have developed into speech acts in which a brief discourse has a typicalized form so that it schematically represents

---

[35] Scholars alternate using 'insults' and the more technical notion of 'face threatening act(s)' or FTA(s), deriving from Brown and Levinson's politeness theory, and indicating any (non-)linguistic act aimed at damaging the self-image and self-preservation of Ss and Hs. For reasons of space, I prefer discussing insults and other synonymic expressions (offences, S-T words, SOTL, etc.) used thus far.

an entire speech event. ... On the semantic level, we distinguish between truth-conditional and performative insults. This distinction is useful in order to distinguish between slanders and slurs, on the one hand, and name-calling and expletives, on the other. ... Furthermore, we distinguish between conventionalized insults and particularized insults. ... Conventionalized insults are those which in normal circumstances are understood as insults by all members of a speech community, e.g. slanderous remarks, contemptuous remarks, name calling, and demeaning expletives. ... Particularized insults, on the other hand, are those which do not have this conventional force. They are more difficult to identify for the analyst because they depend on the reaction of the target to an utterance that does not have this conventional force. ... The dimensions on the next level are concerned with the attitude of the speaker. ... Insults may also be unintentional. ... insults are primarily perlocutionary. An utterance may have the effect of wounding the addressee even if the speaker did not mean to offend him/her. ... The last dimension concerns the reaction of the target. A personal insult requires a denial or an excuse, while a ritual insult requires a response in kind .... Flytings may either end in actual violence or in silence, with which one of the contenders admits his inferiority. (2000: 74–76)

This framework, together with Culpeper's definition of taboo language as one of the possible output strategies of positive impoliteness, and Allan and Burridge's notion of dysphemism comprise the methodological starting point for the lesson plan on insults in *The Taming of the Shrew*. Table 10 summarises the three taxonomies presented in this subsection, with the most relevant aspects for this Element in bold:

The most complete and detailed study of impoliteness in Shakespeare's *The Taming of the Shrew* is undoubtedly Del Villano's *Using the Devil with Courtesy: Shakespeare and the Language of (Im)politeness* (2018), whose last chapter (137–71) is devoted to the gendering of (im)politeness in this Shakespearean comedy. Del Villano divides her study into five sections, focusing on the (im)polite

Table 10 Summary of the main taxonomies adopted in this Element to deal with SOTL (emphases added).

Culpeper (1996: 356–57)	Jucker and Taavitsainen (2000)	Allan and Burridge (2006)
(1) Bald on record impoliteness – the FTA is performed in a direct, clear, unambiguous and concise way in circumstances where face is not irrelevant or minimised. . . .	Pragmatic space of insults: (1) Formal level (2) Semantics (3) Context dependence (4) Speaker attitude (5) Reaction	Socio-cultural framework of taboo language: (1) Orthophemism (straight talking) (2) Euphemism (sweet talking) (3) Dysphemism (speaking offensively)
(2) Positive impoliteness – the use of strategies designed to damage the addressee's positive face wants.		
(3) Negative impoliteness – the use of strategies designed to damage the addressee's negative face wants.		
(4) Sarcasm or mock politeness – the FTA is performed with the use of politeness strategies that are obviously insincere, and thus remain surface realisations. . . .		
(5) Withhold politeness – the absence of politeness work where it would be expected.		

dynamics among the play's characters. A summary of (only) the taboo language used in each section is given in Table 11.

Other examples (adapted from Maturi, 2021: 50–51) of S-T words, insults, and offences in *The Shrew* are as follows:

- PETRUCHIO: Senseless villain (1.2.34)
- HORTENSIO: Twangling Jack (2.1.154)
- PETRUCHIO: you logger-headed . . . foolish knave . . . You peasant swain! You whoreson malt-horse drudge! . . . rascal knaves . . . you rogues, you villains . . . a whoreson, beetle-headed, flap-eared knave! . . . dogs . . . rascal . . . villain (4.1.96–134)
- HORTENSIO: Cullion (4.2.20)
- Other insults repeated more than once by various characters in the play, very common in the early modern period, are (in alphabetical order) *ass, fool, knave, rascal, rogue, and villain*.

Nathalie Vienne-Guerrin has recently analysed insults in *The Taming of the Shrew* and their 'complex dialectics of tongue taming' (2022: 18). Like many other scholars before her (see, among others, Underdown, 1985; Boose, 1991; Ingram, 1994; Bardsley, 2006; Cressy, 2010), Vienne-Guerrin considers that the very first insult in the comedy is in its title:

> In the sixteenth century, the words 'shrew' and 'scold' evoke a social reality, an ideological conception as well as a folkloric and literary type, three essential aspects that Shakespeare integrates into his dramatic work. In Elizabethan times, the shrew is first and foremost a tongue that needs to be controlled. . . . In *The Taming of the Shrew*, Shakespeare reflects his society's attempts and failure to control the excesses of this tongue. (161)

The very title of this comedy thus anticipates the impolite behaviour towards someone whose tongue is too bald and direct – and hence needs to be tamed. As we all know, this is precisely the case of Katherine, 'who goes through a non-naturalistic transformation that leads her to abandon her initial scold-like behaviour and become the perfect example of an obedient wife as a consequence of violent taming by her husband

Table 11 A summary of Del Villano's analysis of taboo language in *The Taming of the Shrew* (2018: 139–70).

Section of *The Shrew* / characters involved	Abusive language (S-T words, SOTL, etc.)
1) The induction: (Im)politeness and identity construction	'HOSTESS: you rogue' (1.1.2); 'SLY: Y'are a baggage' (1.1.3); 'LORD: Thou art a fool . . . O monstrous beast, how like a swine he lies! / Grim death, how foul and loathsome is thine image' (1.1.22; 33–34)
2) Sly, the Lord	–
3) Katherina and Bianca: Impoliteness vs obedience	'KATHERINA: fool' (1.1.65) 'Minion' (2.1.13)
4) Katherina and Petruccio: Introducing mock politeness	PETRUCHIO:[36] 'You wasp' (2.1.205); 'KATHERINA: Fool' (2.1.208); 'a half lunatic; / A mad-cup ruffian and a swearing Jack' (2.1.276–77)
5) The taming	–

Petruccio' (Del Villano, 2018: 138). Although critics discuss the fact that 'Shakespeare's time was a transitional period for a term [*shrew*] that was not yet exclusively reserved for women', Early Modern English was 'a period in which the term was increasingly used in the feminine' (Vienne-Guerrin, 2022: 162). This leads to the consideration that *The Taming of the Shrew* is a privileged field for the investigation of gender relations – and power imbalance, above all – also from a pragmalinguistic point of view. As a matter of fact, after '[h]aving subjected Katherina to every sort of abuse by starving her and denying her clothing, Petruccio's endgame strategy

---

[36] Here I adopt the spelling used in The New Cambridge Shakespeare edition (third ed.) of *The Taming of the Shrew* (ed. A. Thompson, 2017), which is the edition I used to quote from the play. Thus, only act, scene, and line numbers will be quoted in the main text. See references for more details.

focuses on the linguistic power of a husband over his wife' (Del Villano, 2018: 166). As explained by Vienne-Guerrin,

> [d]escribed as 'Katherine the curst' (1.2.127), 'rough' (1.1.55), 'fiend of hell' (1.1.88), 'hell' (1.1.124), 'curst and shrewd' (1.1.179), 'a shrewd, ill-favoured wife' (1.2.59), 'intolerable curst, / And shrewd, and froward' (1.2.88–9), 'an irksome brawling scold' (1.2.186), 'wildcat' (1.2.195), 'thou hilding of a devilish spirit' (2.1.26) or 'this proud disdainful haggard' (4.2.39), associated with the image of Socrates' Xanthippe (1.2.70), Kate (whose surname can be related to 'cat' or 'kite') becomes an imaginary presence. Characters talk about her more than she talks herself and she is recurrently transformed into a tale. Petruccio, on the other hand, proves very noisy and he paradoxically uses insults to tame Kate's unruly tongue. If Kate's insults have no effect on Petruccio, his words of abuse are efficient on her. (2022: 168)

In other words, SOTL in *The Taming of the Shrew* depends on 'pragmatic significance, i.e., their scope, extent and purpose', and putting them in the meaningful context of the Shakespearean text also 'serve(s) to explore the gender [as well as social] dynamics at its heart' (Del Villano, 2018: 171). The following lesson plan, however, assumes the gender-related considerations dealt with in this subsection and focuses on other dynamics, whereby S-T words underline the power imbalance among the characters, that is, the relationship between a master, Petruchio, and his servants.

Lesson Plan 3

Noticing Activity (Input)

Secondary School

Both secondary school and university students will familiarise themselves with the text (4.1.91–138) and, more generally, with the plot and main themes of *The Taming of the Shrew*. Speaking and writing skills will

Enter PETRUCHIO *and* KATHERINA.

PETRUCHIO. Where be these knaves? ...

ALL SERVINGMEN. Here! Here, sir, here, sir!

PETRUCHIO. 'Here sir, here sir, here sir, here, sir!'

You logger-headed and unpolished grooms!

What, no attendance? No regard? No duty?

Where is the foolish knave I sent before?

GRUMIO. Here sir, as foolish as I was before.

PETRUCHIO. You peasant swain! You whoreson malthorse drudge!

Did I not bid thee meet me in the park

And bring along these rascal knaves with thee?

... Go, rascals, go, and fetch my supper in.

                                                      Exeunt Servingmen

... Sit down, Kate, and welcome. Food, food, food, food!

                      Enter Servants with supper.

Why, when, I say? Nay, good sweet Kate, be merry.

Off with my boots, you rogues, you villains! When?

... Out, you rogue! You pluck my foot awry.

Take that!

                        [He strikes the Servant.]

And mend the plucking off the other.

... Where are my slippers? Shall I have some water?

Come, Kate, and wash, and welcome heartily.

You whoreson villain! Will you let it fall?

                        [He strikes the Servant.]

KATHERINA. Patience, I pray you. 'Twas a fault unwilling.

PETRUCHIO. A whoreson beetle-headed, flap-eared knave!

Come, Kate, sit down; I know you have a stomach.

Will you give thanks, sweet Kate, or else shall I?

What's this? Mutton?

FIRST SERVINGMAN. Ay.

PETRUCHIO. 'Tis burnt, and so is all the meat.

What dogs are these! Where is the rascal cook?

How durst you villains bring it from the dresser

And serve it thus to me that love it no?

There, take it to you, trenchers, cups and all!

                 [He throws the food and dishes at them.]

You heedless joltheads and unmannered slaves!

What, do you grumble? I'll be with you straight.

                               [Exeunt Servants]

                                 (4.1.91–138)

Phases	Secondary School Students	University Students
Noticing activity (Input)	• The teacher may help students by introducing the plot and main themes of *The Taming of the Shrew* with particular emphasis on this scene, and the 'strange' aggressive behaviour adopted by Petruchio (the Cambridge School Shakespeare book series can be useful at this stage; see Brady, 2014). • A short clip of the scene is shown (see next paragraph for details) and students are invited to guess the power relationship among the characters onstage, in order to understand Ss' and Hs' reactions to SOTL (brainstorming activity). • S-T words are highlighted in the text.	• Students read the text by themselves and guess the power relations among the characters onstage. Once they are familiar with the play, they can also read Ann Thompson's introduction to The New Cambridge Shakespeare edition of *The Taming of the Shrew* (2017: 1–58) as an assignment. • Students are introduced to the field of (im)politeness, and taboo language in particular (Culpeper, 1996, 2018; Jucker and Taavitsainen, 2000; Allan and Burridge, 2006; Del Villano, 2018). Special attention should be paid to gender and social rank issues.
Awareness activity (Scaffolding I)	A written or computer-based drag-and-drop exercise is provided where students combine a series (2+) of adjectives and a noun, in order to explore the syntactic and lexical creativeness (Jucker and Taavitsainen, 2000: 74) of Shakespearean insults in *The Shrew*.	By referring to Jucker and Taavitsainen's pragmatic space of insults (2000: 74, 2008: 6), students will classify the text's taboo language and dysphemisms.

	Possible modern versions or L1 translations are provided with the help of a dictionary.	
Guided practice (Scaffolding II)	A rephrasing exercise is given (again, written or computer-based) where students are asked to write possible polite versions of the insults provided.	To prepare for the autonomous practice phase, students will write lists of counts against Petruchio by paraphrasing the insults he hurled at Grumio and the other subordinates. Power imbalance relations should be highlighted in order to convince a hypothetical jury in the following phase of the lesson plan.
Autonomous practice (Output)	Students will work in pairs. A TikTok challenge will be launched called 'How to do things with (other) words'. One student records a short TikTok video with bleeped insults and the other responds with another TikTok playing an attenuated, polite version of his/her colleague's video, maintaining the same pragmatic, communicative intent.	Working in groups, an early modern courtroom will be set up. Katherina, Grumio, and all the servants will bring charges against Petruchio because of the insults he hurled at them. A judge will decide on the gravity of the facts and condemn or absolve Petruchio.

be elicited during this first phase. The teacher may help younger students by introducing the play, emphasising the main linguistic and content-related characteristics of the scene considered. The Cambridge School Shakespeare book series can be a useful resource at this stage (Brady, 2014). In particular, Petruchio's aggressive language deserves attention (a good explanation is provided at www.youtube.com/watch?v=nuBb-0p5u2c). After that, a short clip of the scene is shown; for example, 4.1 from Lucy Bailey's 2012 RSC production is recommended, since the latest productions (Fentiman's 2014 and

Audibert's 2019) present a provocative gender-swapped world that may be too distant from the aims of this lesson plan. A brief brainstorming activity follows (with the support of the blackboard or online interactive boards such as Webwhiteboard by Miro): students are invited to guess the power relationship among the characters onstage in order to understand the Ss' and Hs' reactions to SOTL. An example of a brainstorming activity is given in Figure 7.

S-T words are highlighted in the text and inserted in the brainstorming.

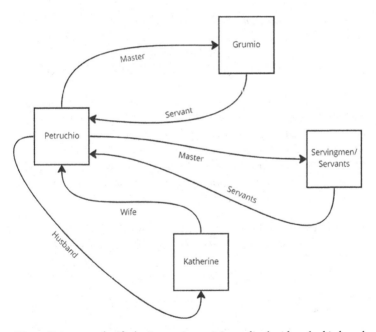

Figure 7 An example of a brainstorming activity realised with webwhiteboard .com by Miro.

University

University students, on the other hand, will read the text by themselves and interpret the different roles (role play) and guess the power relations among the characters onstage. Once they are familiar with the play, they can also study Thompson's introduction to The New Cambridge Shakespeare edition of *The Taming of the Shrew* (2017: 1–58) as an assignment. The lecturer introduces them to Culpeper's model of impoliteness (1996 and ff.) and to the relationship between taboo language and impoliteness (Jucker and Taavitsainen, 2000; Allan and Burridge, 2006; Culpeper, 2018). Special attention should be paid to gender and social rank issues (Del Villano, 2018).

Awareness Activity (Scaffolding I)

Secondary School

Secondary school pupils will be assigned a written or computer-based drag-and-drop exercise where two or more adjectives (or adjectival nouns/phrases) and nouns, which compose creative insults in Early Modern English (see Figure 8), are given in random order. In this way, the syntactic and lexical creativity (Jucker and Taavitsainen, 2000: 74) of Shakespearean insults in *The Shrew* is explored. Possible modern versions or L1 translations are provided with the help of a dictionary or through websites such as the Shakespearean insults generator (www.librariesha

Figure 8 An example of a reordering drag-and-drop exercise realised with classtools.net (www.classtools.net/dragdrop/).

waii.org/learn/brain-games/bardly-barbs/) or the Shakespeare insult kit (www.scholastic.com/content/dam/teachers/articles/migrated-files-in-body/shakespeare_insult_kit.pdf), which draws on Rex Gibson's list of Shakespearean insults (1998: 197–99).

University

On the other hand, by referring to Jucker and Taavitsainen's pragmatic space of insults (2000: 74, 2008: 6), university students will classify the taboo language and dysphemisms in the text, analysing them in terms of formal level, semantics, context dependence, speaker attribute, and H's reaction.

Guided Practice (Scaffolding II)

Secondary School

A rephrasing exercise is given to secondary school students (again, written or computer-based). They are required to write alternative versions of the insults provided, toning them down (e.g., 'you whoreson villain' = 'you are a contemptible bad person'). Both versions should be considered in preparation of the final output.

University

University students, on the other hand, will be asked to write down a list of indictments against Petruchio by paraphrasing the insults he uttered against his servants. Power imbalance relations should be underlined in order to convince a hypothetical jury in the following phase of the lesson plan. An example of a list of indictments is given as follows:

1) Harassment: The master hit his servants because they let some water fall on the ground.
2) Calumny: The master hurled insults and offences at his servants because they did not remove his boots
3) ...

Autonomous Practice (Output)

Secondary School

The autonomous phase will focus on spoken interaction (after two written activities in the scaffolding part). Secondary school students will launch a TikTok challenge entitled 'How to do things with (other) words' (to paraphrase Austin's well-known milestone collection of lectures). They will work in pairs and record double videos. One student records a TikTok by imitating Petruchio, but bleeping the SOTL, while another records another TikTok, which is a toned-down version of his/her colleague's video. What is important is to maintain the same pragmatic and communicative intent. If constraints such as space, equipment, or school regulations prevent students from finishing their task in class, they have the option to complete it at home.

University

University students will also exploit cooperative learning, but work in groups rather than pairs. An imaginary early modern courtroom will be set up with a judge, a prosecutor, a defence lawyer, Petruchio, Katherina, Grumio, and other serving men. Katherina, Grumio, and all the servants will play the prosecution, while Petruchio plays the defence. Charges will be pressed on the basis of the S-T words employed by Petruchio in 4.1. The judge will decide on the gravity of the facts and condemn or absolve Petruchio, also referring to the pragmatics space of insults by Jucker and Taavitsainen, that is, deciding on the semantic force of the offence, the speaker's attitude, and the addressees' reactions.

Conclusion

A Preliminary Experiment with Shakespeare as CBLT in the ESL Classroom

'A book about Shakespeare which reduces his great literary masterpieces to mere tools for teaching a foreign language? Scandalous!' (Dobson, 2017: vii). Michael Dobson's provocative incipit to his preface in Lau and Tso's *Teaching Shakespeare to ESL Students* ironically comments on the tone of this Element as well. I hope that the previous sections have demonstrated that teaching English as a FL via Shakespeare's plays is definitely not a 'scandalous' reduction of his literary output. On the contrary, in my view, it is one of the most productive ways of exploiting the linguistic potentials intrinsically offered by works that have contributed so much to shaping the English language as we know and use it today. Paraphrasing Jan Kott's[37] most famous book, it is also a way to make 'Shakespeare our contemporary' (1964).

Furthermore, the prevalence of literature addressing the teaching of English with Shakespeare in non-Anglophone countries, as evidenced by works such as Lau and Tso (2017) and others including Michael Flachmann (1997), Todd Heyden (2002), Christiane Lütge and Maria Eisenmann (2014), Tso (2016), and Kohei Uchimaru (2020), underscores the enduring significance of Shakespeare as a ubiquitous figure in ESL syllabi. This trend not only emphasises his pervasive presence but also fuels the ongoing discourse regarding adaptations, reworking, simplifications, modernisations, and other pedagogical approaches associated with Shakespeare's works. What is 'scandalous', some critics may argue, is the oversimplification of Shakespeare's language, especially when teaching primary school pupils or novice adult learners.

Of course, extreme attempts to modernise Shakespeare's Early Modern English are absolutely respectable and extremely useful for their intended readers (e.g., foreigners who approach Shakespeare for the first time, very young learners, among others). However, given the purpose of this Element, these intralinguistic translations of Shakespeare plays were not particularly useful. As a matter of fact, this Element has tried to demonstrate that once spelling modernisation has been carried out, the main morphosyntactic and lexical difficulties with a 500-year-old language can be overcome using specialised dictionaries[38] or glossed editions of the texts, given

---

[37] Actually, it was the English translator of Kott's book, i.e., Bolesław Taborski, who 'invented' this title in 1964. The original Polish title (1961) is *Szkice o Szekspirze* (lit. 'Sketches about Shakespeare').

[38] On the topic of specialised dictionaries, it is worth mentioning LEME (Lexicons of Early Modern English, available at https://leme.library.utoronto.ca).

the huge amount of material available on Shakespeare. This triggers a pedagogical virtuous circle whereby the more material that is produced for ESL instructors and learners about Shakespeare in the English language classroom, the more his plays are known and exploited in educational environments worldwide, the more Shakespeare-centred pedagogical experiences and experiments produce outcomes which in turn become teaching materials.

As for the specific level of linguistic analysis, this Element has aimed to go beyond considerations of spelling, grammar, and vocabulary. Its purpose is to use Shakespeare's plays (in particular *Richard III*, *Romeo and Juliet*, and *The Taming of the Shrew*) to teach English pragmatics – with a specific focus on speech act theory, DMs, and (im)politeness strategies – a 'somewhat neglected or marginalized' (Ivanova, 2018: 27) field of language pedagogies, although '[r]esearch of the past three decades has shown almost unanimously that the teaching of pragmatic skills to language learners is not only feasible … and desirable …, but also more effective than mere exposure to the target language' (Glaser, 2013: 151). Nevertheless, linguistic interfaces are carefully considered and treated, so that when dealing with pragmatics, interfaces with morphosyntax and lexis are dealt with. In this Element, Shakespeare's plays are used both as linguistic means and literary content in what has been defined as CBLT or CBI. Literature as content offers a number of topics and themes to be combined with metalinguistic reflection (LLE) with the final goal of creating useful ready-made lesson plans to be implemented in both secondary school and university ESL courses. In fact, the model proposed to deliver both ESL secondary school classes and university lectures using Shakespeare's plays is Lyster's (2018) four-phased proactive approach – that is, (1) noticing activity phase; (2)

Currently based at the University of Toronto, Canada, LEME contains 1,162,192 total word entries from 1,466 lexical texts (monolingual/bilingual dictionaries, glossaries, lists, tables, etc.) dating from 1475, when William Caxton established the first English printing press in London, to 1755, when Samuel Johnson published his well-known *Dictionary*. Lexicons of Early Modern English is a valuable source for researchers, teachers, and learners of English who are interested in Early Modern English.

awareness activity phase; (3) guided practice phase; and (4) autonomous practice phase – which he created for the specific purposes of CBLT. By transforming the traditional tripartite model of lesson plans (input, scaffolding, output), Lyster's approach allows teachers and lecturers to focus more on the linguistic training of learners, since the scaffolding phase – which in CBLT is the core of the teaching of specific/specialised language of a non-linguistic discipline – is split in two, in order to give instructors and students more space and time to acquire linguistic structures.

In Section 1, curses from *Richard III* offer much food for thought for a lesson plan about speech acts in Shakespeare's plays and their implementation as pragmatic devices in the ESL classroom, with particular attention to female characters and men–women power imbalance. Using act 4, scene 1 as input – a dialogue between Lady Anne (widow of the late Edward, Prince of Wales, and now wife-to-be of Richard), Queen Elizabeth (wife to late Edward IV), and the Duchess of York (his mother and mother of Richard) – both secondary school and university students are encouraged to work on their speaking skills. Younger students enact a role play whose protagonists were Anne, Elizabeth, and the Duchess, trying to use as many kinds of speech acts as possible. Elizabeth and the Duchess are TV talk show presenters and interview the future queen Anne, who has just heard the news of her imminent coronation. University students prepare PowerPoint or Prezi presentations on the pragmalinguistic representation of female feelings and emotions in *Richard III*, highlighting the pivotal role of expressive performative speech acts, to be presented and discussed with their peers in a seminar-like format.

Section 2, which focuses on *Romeo and Juliet*, examines a dialogue between the Nurse, Peter, and Romeo from 2.4 about arrangements for Romeo and Juliet's secret marriage. Exploiting the communicative potential of DMs in the scene, both secondary school and university students are invited to work on their writing skills. On the one hand, secondary school students are required to create WhatsApp groups with the Nurse, Peter, and Romeo as members and must arrange the marriage Friar Lawrence has accepted to celebrate. Of course, given the focus on DMs, their use is elicited during the output phase. On the other hand, university students are asked to write (in)formal letters to characters in the play, inviting them to the ceremony. In this case, DMs are to be used to set the tone and register of the letters.

Lastly, in Section 3, *The Taming of the Shrew*, 4.1 is selected as the privileged field to investigate (im)politeness strategies such as insults, offences, and taboo language, with the firm belief that aggressive language should be taught in the ESL classroom, at least to ensure students avoid it in certain communicative contexts. A combination of speaking and writing skills is elicited. Secondary school students launch a TikTok challenge, recording short double videos with bleeped insults, on the one hand, and their attenuated, polite versions on the other. In the university lecture, however, an early modern courtroom can be set up, with Katherina, Grumio, and all the servants accusing Petruchio of hurling insults at his subordinates. A student playing the judge must decide on the gravity of the facts and condemn or absolve Petruchio.

This Element offers merely a preliminary exploration of the many ways Shakespeare's plays can be used in the ESL classroom to teach English pragmatics. Firstly, the corpus of texts considered could easily be expanded and the entire Shakespearean corpus investigated, even to find recurring pragmatic patterns and features. Secondly, other pragmatic and pragmalinguistic areas could be taken into account, such as deictics, implicatures, and presuppositions, to mention only a few. A larger-scale theoretical project, which is beyond the scope of this Element, would certainly benefit from the tools offered by corpus pragmatics (see Aijmer and Rühlemann, 2015; Taavitsainen et al., 2015; Weisser, 2018, 2020), a transdisciplinary field of study which combines pragmatics and corpus linguistics, thus giving scholars the possibility of managing large amounts of data (in this case texts and words), and which has recently received critical attention in Shakespeare studies (see, among others, Mullini, 2016; Culpeper and Oliver, 2020; Oliver, 2022).

All things considered, this Element has merely scratched the surface of a very rich and vastly unexplored field of research, which warrants scholarly attention not only to understand the linguistic (especially pragmatic) mechanisms of Early Modern English and, above all, Shakespeare's language but also to improve and expand research into Shakespeare and the pedagogy of the English language in the ESL classroom. Almost 500 years later, Shakespeare's plays still have a great deal to tell us, also from a linguistic viewpoint.

Glossary

Collocational pattern(ing):   The pattern of habitual juxtaposition of a particular word with another word or words with a frequency greater than chance.

Communicative approach: An approach to language teaching that emphasises communication as both the goal and the means of instruction.

Constructivism: A learning theory and philosophical approach that suggests learners actively construct their own understanding and knowledge of the world through their experiences and interactions.

Corpus-based: An approach or methodology that relies on the analysis of large and structured collections of texts that serve as representative samples of a language or a specific domain.

Diachrony: Referring to the study or analysis of language changes and developments over time.

Functionalism: A theoretical approach that emphasises the communicative functions of language and the role of language in serving the needs of its users within a particular social context.

Grammar-translation approach: A traditional method of language teaching that dates back to the nineteenth century. It was widely used for teaching classical languages such as Latin and ancient Greek, but it has also been applied to the teaching of modern languages. It has been criticised for its lack of emphasis on communication and real-life language use.

Grammaticalisation:
The transformation of lexemes (words with specific meanings) into grammatical elements (such as particles, prepositions, or inflections) that serve to indicate relationships between words in a sentence or convey grammatical features.

Hypernym:
A word that represents a broader or more general category that encompasses other, more specific members, called hyponyms (e.g., *animal* is the hypernym, *dog* is its hyponym).

Lemma:
The base or dictionary form of a word, often the form under which it is listed in a dictionary.

Lexicalisation:
The process by which a word or a group of words acquires a specific meaning, often in a context-specific or idiomatic manner. It involves the incorporation of new lexical items or the modification of existing ones to express a particular concept, idea, or meaning.

Lexico-pragmatics (lexical pragmatics):
A study area that aims to systematically explain how language use is influenced by the meaning of words, focusing on the connection between semantics and pragmatic aspects.

Metacomment:
A comment or statement within a piece of communication that reflects on or explains the communication itself.

Morphosyntax:
The study of the interaction between morphological and syntactic elements in a language. In other words, morphosyntax explores how the structure and formation of words (morphology) interact with the structure of sentences and phrases (syntax).

PoS tag(ging):	A technique that involves assigning a specific grammatical category, or PoS, to each word in a given text. The parts of speech include nouns, verbs, adjectives, adverbs, pronouns, prepositions, conjunctions, and interjections.
Pragmalinguistics:	A field of study that encompasses the pragmatic study of a language.
Pragmaticalisation:	A process in the evolution of language, particularly regarding how it is used in discourse, leading to linguistic units that once held specific meanings now taking on purely pragmatic functions in communication.
Prescriptivism:	A viewpoint that emphasises adhering to established language rules, norms, and conventions.
Sociopragmatics:	A field of study that examines the social aspects of language usage.
Structuralism:	A theoretical approach that emerged in the early twentieth century, particularly associated with the work of Swiss linguist Ferdinand de Saussure. This approach focuses on analysing language as a structured system of elements and relationships, emphasising the study of the internal structures and rules that govern language.
Synchrony:	The study or analysis of a language or linguistic phenomenon at a specific point in time, without considering its historical development or changes.

References

Adams, M. (2002). 'Teaching "Bad" American English'. *Journal of English Linguistics*, 30(4), 353–65.

Aijmer, K. (1997). '"I Think" – An English Modal Particle'. In T. Swan & O. J. Westvik, eds., *Modality in Germanic Languages: Historical and Comparative Perspectives*. Berlin: de Gruyter, pp. 1–47.

Aijmer, K. & Rühlemann, C., eds. (2015). *Corpus Pragmatics: A Handbook*. Cambridge: Cambridge University Press.

Allan, K. & Burridge, K. (2006). *Forbidden Words: Taboo and the Censoring of Language*. Cambridge: Cambridge University Press.

Arafah, B. (2018). 'Incorporating the Use of Literature as an Innovative Technique for Teaching English'. *AICLL*, 1, 24–36.

Arnovik, L. (1999). *Diachronic Pragmatics: Seven Case Studies in English Illocutionary Development*. Amsterdam: John Benjamins.

Anderson, L. W. & Krathwohl, D. R., eds. (2001). *A Taxonomy for Learning, Teaching, and Assessing: A Revision of Bloom's Taxonomy of Educational Objectives*. Boston: Allyn & Bacon.

Aston, R. J. (2020). *The Role of Literary Canon in the Teaching of Literature*. New York: Routledge.

Atmaca, H. & Günday, R. (2016). 'Using Literary Texts to Teach Grammar in Foreign Language Classroom'. *Participatory Educational Research*, Special Issue 2016–IV, 127–33.

Austin, J. L. (1962). *How to Do Things with Words*. Oxford: Clarendon Press.

Austin, P. (1990). 'Politeness Revisited – The Dark Side'. In A. Bell & J. Holmes, eds., *New Zealand Ways of Speaking English*. Bristol: Multilingual Matters, pp. 276–94.

Bardsley, S. (2006). *Venomous Tongues: Speech and Gender in Late Medieval England*. Philadelphia: University of Pennsylvania Press.

Bassnett, S. & Grundy, P. (1993). *Language through Literature*. London: Longman.

Bauer, M., Glaesser, J., Kelava, A., Kirchhoff, L., & Zirker, A. (2022). '"When Most I Wink, then" – What? Assessing the Comprehension of Literary Texts in University Students of English as a Second Language'. *Language and Literature*, 31(3), 1–20.

Beeching, K. (2016). *Pragmatic Markers in British English – Meaning in Social Interaction*. Cambridge: Cambridge University Press.

Bertuccelli Papi, M. (2000). 'Is a Diachronic Speech Act Theory Possible?' *Journal of Historical Pragmatics*, 1(1), 57–66.

Blakemore, D. (1987). *Semantic Constraints on Relevance*. Oxford: Blackwell.

Blakemore, D. (2002). *Relevance and Linguistic Meaning: The Semantics and Pragmatics of Discourse Markers*. Cambridge: Cambridge University Press.

Blakemore Evans, G., ed. (2018). *The New Cambridge Shakespeare: Romeo and Juliet*, updated ed. Cambridge: Cambridge University Press.

Blank, P. (2018). *Shakesplish: How We Read Shakespeare's Language*. Stanford: Stanford University Press.

Bobkina, J. (2014). 'The Use of Literature and Literary Texts in the EFL Classroom: Between Consensus and Controversy'. *International Journal of Applied Linguistics & English Literature*, 3(2), 248–60.

Boose, L. E. (1991). 'Scolding Brides and Bridling Scolds: Taming the Woman's Unruly Member'. *Shakespeare Quarterly*, 41(2), 179–213.

Bousfield, D. (2008). *Impoliteness in Interaction*. Amsterdam: John Benjamins.

Bousfield, D. & Culpeper, J. (2008). 'Impoliteness: Eclecticism and Diaspora'. *Journal of Politeness Research*, 4(2), 161–68.

Bowles, H. & Murphy, A. (2020). *English-Medium Instruction and the Internationalization of Universities*. Cham: Palgrave Macmillan.

Brady, L. (2014). *Cambridge School Shakespeare: The Taming of the Shrew*, 3rd ed. Cambridge: Cambridge University Press.

Brady, L. & Coles, J., eds. (2018). *Cambridge School Shakespeare: King Richard III*, 3rd ed. Cambridge: Cambridge University Press.

Brinton, D., Snow, M., & Wesche, M. (1989). *Content-Based Second Language Instruction*. New York: Newbury House.

Brinton, L. J. (1990). 'The Development of Discourse Markers in English'. In J. Fisiak, ed., *Historical Linguistics and Philology*. Berlin: de Gruyter, pp. 45–71.

Brinton, L. J. (1996). *Pragmatic Markers in English: Grammaticalization and Discourse Functions*. Berlin: de Gruyter.

Brinton, L. J. (2007). 'The Development of I Mean: Implications for the Study of Historical Pragmatics'. In S. M. Fitzmaurice & I. Taavitsainen, eds., *Methods in Historical Pragmatics*. Berlin: de Gruyter, pp. 37–80.

Brinton, L. J. (2010). 'Discourse Markers'. In A. H. Jucker & I. Taavitsainen, eds., *Historical Pragmatics*. Berlin: de Gruyter, pp. 285–314.

Brosa Rodríguez, A. (2021). 'Corpus and Universals in Language in Pragmatics'. *e-AESLA*, 7, 37–49.

Brown, G. & Yule, G. (1983). *Discourse Analysis*. Cambridge: Cambridge University Press.

Brown, P. & Levinson, S. C. (1978/1987). *Politeness: Some Universals in Language Use*. Cambridge: Cambridge University Press.

Bruner, J. S. (1983). 'The Acquisition of Pragmatic Commitments'. In R. Golinkoff, ed., *The Transition from Prelinguistic to Linguistic Communication*. Hillsdale: Erlbaum, pp. 27–42.

Bruti, S. (2016). 'Teaching Compliments and Insults in the EFL Classroom through Film Clips'. In F. Bianchi & S. Gesuato, eds., *Pragmatic Issues in Specialized Communicative Contexts*. Leiden: Brill, pp. 149–70.

Busse, B. & Busse, U. (2012). 'Methodological Suggestions for Investigating Shakespearean Discourse Markers on the Old Texts of Shakespeare's Plays'. In C. Suhr & I. Taavitsainen, eds., *Developing*

Corpus Methodology for Historical Pragmatics. Helsinki: University of Helsinki, https://varieng.helsinki.fi/series/volumes/11/busse_busse/#_ftn1 [Accessed 15/1/2023].

Busse, U. & Busse, B. (2017). 'The Language of Shakespeare'. In A. Bergs & L. J. Brinton, eds., *The History of English*, vol. 4: Early Modern English. Berlin: de Gruyter, pp. 309–32.

Butler, J. (1999). *Gender Trouble: Feminism and the Subversion of Identity*. New York: Routledge.

Carter, R. & Long, M. N. (1987). *The Web of Words: Exploring Literature through Language*. Cambridge: Cambridge University Press.

Catasso, N., Coniglio, M., & De Bastiani, C., eds. (2022). *Language Change at the Interfaces: Intrasentential and Intersentential Phenomena*. Amsterdam: John Benjamins.

Charnes, L. (1993). *Notorious Identity: Materializing the Subject in Shakespeare*. Cambridge, MA: Harvard University Press.

Ciambella, F. (2021). 'Training Would-Be Teachers: Premises and Results of a Content-Based ESL Course'. *Status Quaestionis*, 20, 343–69.

Cinganotto, L. (2019). 'Debate as a Teaching Strategy for Language Learning'. *Lingue e Linguaggi*, 30, 107–25.

Corder, S. P. (1967). 'The Significance of Learner's Errors'. *International Review of Applied Linguistics in Language Teaching*, 5(1–4), 161–70.

Coyle, D., Hood, P., & Marsh, D. (2010). *CLIL: Content and Language Integrated Learning*. Cambridge: Cambridge University Press.

Cressy, D. (2010). *Dangerous Talk: Scandalous, Seditious, and Treasonable Speech in Pre-modern England*. Oxford: Oxford University Press.

Crible, L. (2017). 'Towards an Operational Category of Discourse Markers: A Definition and Its Model'. In C. Fedriani & A. Sansò, eds., *Pragmatic Markers, Discourse Markers and Modal Particles: New Perspectives*. Amsterdam: John Benjamins, pp. 97–124.

Crystal, D. (2002). 'To Modernize or Not to Modernize: There Is No Question'. *Groundlingo*, 15–17, www.davidcrystal.com/Files/BooksAnd Articles/-4232.pdf [Accessed 10/8/2022].

Crystal, D. (2012). *'Think on My Words': Exploring Shakespeare's Language*. Cambridge: Cambridge University Press.

Crystal, D. & Crystal, B. (2002). 'Discourse Markers'. *Shakespeare's Words*, www.shakespeareswords.com/Public/LanguageCompanion/ThemesAnd Topics.aspx?TopicId=11 [Accessed 13 February 2023].

Culpeper, J. (1996). 'Towards an Anatomy of Impoliteness'. *Journal of Pragmatics*, 25, 349–67.

Culpeper, J. (2007). 'A New Kind of Dictionary for Shakespeare's Plays: An Immodest Proposal'. *Sederi*, 17, 47–73.

Culpeper, J. (2009). 'Keyness: Words, Parts-of-Speech and Semantic Categories in the Character-Talk of Shakespeare's *Romeo and Juliet*'. *International Journal of Corpus Linguistics*, 14(1), 29–59.

Culpeper, J. (2011). *Impoliteness: Using Language to Cause Offence*. Cambridge: Cambridge University Press.

Culpeper, J. (2011). 'Politeness and Impoliteness'. In K. Aijmer & G. Andersen, eds., *Handbook of Pragmatics*. Berlin: de Gruyter, pp. 391–436.

Culpeper, J. (2014). 'Developing Keyness and Characterization: Annotation'. In D. L. Hoover, J. Culpeper, & K. O'Halloran, eds., *Digital Literary Studies: Corpus Approaches to Poetry, Prose, and Drama*. New York: Routledge, pp. 35–63.

Culpeper, J. (2016). 'Impoliteness Strategies'. In A. Capone & J. L. Mey, eds., *Interdisciplinary Studies in Pragmatics, Culture and Society*. Cham: Springer, pp. 421–46.

Culpeper, J. (2018). 'Taboo Language and Impoliteness'. In K. Allan, ed., *The Oxford Handbook of Taboo Words and Language*. Oxford: Oxford University Press, pp. 28–40.

Culpeper, J. (2021). 'Impoliteness and Hate Speech: Compare and Contrast'. *Journal of Pragmatics*, 179, 4–11.

Culpeper, J. & Hardaker, C. (2017) 'Impoliteness'. In J. Culpeper, M. Haugh, & D. Kadar, eds., *Palgrave Handbook of (Im)politeness*. Basingstoke: Palgrave Macmillan, pp. 199–225.

Culpeper, J. & Haugh, M. (2014). *Pragmatics and the English Language*. Basingstoke: Palgrave Macmillan.

Culpeper, J. & Kytö, M. (2010). *Early Modern English Dialogues: Spoken Interaction as Writing*. Cambridge: Cambridge University Press.

Culpeper, J. & Oliver, S. J. (2020). 'Pragmatic Noise in Shakespeare's Plays'. In E. Jonsson & T. Larsson, eds., *Voices Past and Present – Studies of Involved, Speech-Related and Spoken Texts: In Honor of Merja Kytö*. Amsterdam: John Benjamins, pp. 11–30.

Culpeper, J. & Semino, E. (2000). 'Constructing Witches and Spells: Speech Acts and Activity Types in Early Modern England'. *Journal of Historical Pragmatics*, 1(1), 1–19.

De Klerk, V. (1991). 'Expletives: Men Only?' *Communication Monographs*, 58,156–69.

Degand, L., Cornillie, B., & Pietrandrea, P., eds. (2013). *Discourse Markers and Modal Particles: Categorization and Description*. Amsterdam: John Benjamins, eds.

Del Villano, B. (2018). *Using the Devil with Courtesy: Shakespeare and the Language of (Im)politeness*. Frankfurt am Main: Peter Lang.

Dewaele, J.-M. (2007). 'Context and L2 Users' Pragmatic Development'. In Z. Hua, P. Seedhouse, L. Wei, & V. Cook, eds., *Language Learning and Teaching as Social Inter-Action*. London: Palgrave Macmillan, pp. 163–82.

Dewi, S. U. (2015). 'Syllabus of Vocational Secondary School Based on ESP Approach'. *Dinamika Ilmu*, 15(2), 273–95.

Dhanapal, S. (2010). 'Stylistics and Reader Response: An Integrated Approach to the Teaching of Literary Texts'. *Literacy Information and Computer Education Journal*, 1(4), 233–40.

Divsar, H. & Tahriri, A. (2009). 'Investigating the Effectiveness of an Integrated Approach to Teaching Literature in an EFL Context'. *Pan-Pacific Association of Applied Linguistics*, 2(13), 105–16.

Dobson, M. (2017). 'Preface: Shakespeare and the Teaching of Language'. In L. C. M. Lau & W. B. A. Tso, eds., *Teaching Shakespeare to ESL Students*. Singapore: Springer, pp. vii–ix.

Duff, A. & Maley, A. (1990). *Literature*. Oxford: Oxford University Press.

Dupuis, M. & Tiffany, G., eds. (2013). *Approaches to Teaching Shakespeare's The Taming of the Shrew*. New York: The Modern Language Association of America.

Dusinberre, J. (1996). *Shakespeare and the Nature of Women*. London: Macmillan.

Eisenmann, M. & Lütge, C., eds. (2014). *Shakespeare in the EFL Classroom*. Heidelberg: Universitätsverlag.

Elam, K. (2002). *The Semiotics of Theatre and Drama*, 2nd ed. New York: Routledge.

Elyasi, J. (2013). 'Teaching Language through Literature: A Content-based Instruction Model.' *Journal of Academic and Applied Studies*, 3(10), 9–18.

Estill, L. (2006). 'Performative Language in Renaissance Performance'. http://homes.chass.utoronto.ca/~cpercy/courses/6362-estill.htm [Accessed 16/3/2023].

Farahani, M. V. & Ghane, Z. (2022). 'Unpacking the Function(s) of Discourse Markers in Academic Spoken English: A Corpus-Based Study'. *The Australian Journal of Language and Literacy*, 45, 49–70.

Fedriani, C. & Sansò, A. (2017). *Pragmatic Markers, Discourse Markers and Modal Particles: New Perspectives*. Amsterdam: John Benjamins.

Félix-Brasdefer, J. C. & Cohen, A. D. (2012). 'Teaching Pragmatics in the Foreign Language Classroom: Grammar as a Communicative Resource'. *Hispania*, 95(4), 650–69.

Fenn, R. & McGlynn, A. (2018). *Teaching Grammar through Literature: Bringing Language to Life in the Secondary Classroom*. London: Routledge.

Findlay, A. (2010). *Women in Shakespeare: A Dictionary*. London: Bloomsbury.

Fitzmaurice, S. M. & Taavitsainen, I., eds., (2008). *Methods in Historical Pragmatics*. Berlin: de Gruyter, 37–79.

Flachmann, M. (1997). 'Professional Theater People and English Teachers: Working Together to Teach Shakespeare'. In R. E. Salomone & J. E. Davis, eds., *Teaching Shakespeare: Into the Twenty-First Century*. Athens: Ohio University Press, pp. 57–64.

Fraser, B. (1998). 'Contrastive Discourse Markers in English'. In A. Jucker & Y. Ziv, eds., *Discourse Markers: Description and Theory*. Amsterdam: John Benjamins, pp. 301–26.

Fraser, B. (2006). 'On the Conceptual-Procedural Distinction'. *Style*, 40(1–2), 24–32.

Fraser, B. (2009). 'An Account of Discourse Markers'. *International Review of Pragmatics*, 1(2), 293–320.

Fraser, B. (2009). 'Topic Orientation Markers'. *Journal of Pragmatics*, 41(5), 892–98.

Furkó, P. (2014). 'Cooptation over Grammaticalization – The Characteristics of Discourse Markers Reconsidered'. *Argumentum*, 10, 289–300.

Furkó, P. (2018). 'The Boundaries of Discourse Markers – Drawing Lines through Manual and Automatic Annotation'. *Acta Universitatis Sapientiae, Philologica*, 10(2), 155–70.

Ghezzi, C. (2014). 'The Development of Discourse and Pragmatic Markers'. In C. Ghezzi & P. Molinelli, eds., *Discourse and Pragmatic Markers from Latin to the Romance Languages*. Oxford: Oxford University Press, pp. 10–26.

Ghezzi, C. Jr. (2024). 'Compliments, Insults, and Broken Taboos in Richard III's Quest for Power'. In F. Ciambella, ed., *Taboo Language and (Im)politeness in Early Modern English Drama*. Naples: UniorPress, pp. 21–57.

Gibson, R. (1998). *Teaching Shakespeare: A Handbook for Teachers*. Cambridge: Cambridge University Press.

Gilfillan Upton, B. (2006). *Hearing Mark's Endings: Listening to Ancient Popular Texts through Speech Act Theory*. Leiden: Brill.

Glaser, K. (2013). 'The Neglected Combination: A Case for Explicit-Inductive Instruction in Teaching Pragmatics in ESL'. *TESL Canada Journal*, 30(7), 150–63.

Goffman, E. (1967). *Interaction Ritual: Essays in Face-to-Face Behavior*. Chicago: Aldine.

Gotti, M. (2003). *Specialized Discourse: Linguistic Features and Changing Conventions*. Bern: Peter Lang.

Grice, H. P. (1968). 'Utterer's Meaning, Sentence-Meaning, and Word-Meaning'. *Foundations of Language*, 4(3), 225–42.

Grice, H. P. (1975). 'Logic and Conversation'. In P. Cole & J. J. Morgan, eds., *Syntax and Semantics 3: Speech Acts*. New York: Academic Press, pp. 41–58.

Hall, G. (2015). *Literature in Language Education*, 2nd ed. Basingstoke: Palgrave Macmillan.

Hamamra, B. (2019). 'Performative Utterances and Gender Performance in Shakespeare's *Richard III*'. *Bethlehem University Journal*, 36, 115–32.

Hansen, M.-B. M. (1997). '*Alors* and *Donc* in Spoken French: A Reanalysis'. *Journal of Pragmatics*, 28, 153–87.

Hansen, M.-B. M. (2006). 'A Dynamic Polysemy Approach to the Lexical Semantics of Discourse Markers (With an Exemplary Analysis of French "Toujours")'. In K. Fischer, ed., *Approaches to Discourse Particles*. Amsterdam: Elsevier, pp. 21–41.

Harrabi, A. (2011). 'ESP Education in Tunisia: The Way for a Reform'. In A. Shafaei, ed., *Frontiers of Language and Teaching*, vol. 2. Boca Raton: Brown Walker Press, pp. 166–71.

He, P., & Lin, A. (2018). 'Becoming a "Language-Aware" Content Teacher: Content and Language Integrated Learning (CLIL) Teacher Professional Development as a Collaborative, Dynamic, and Dialogic Process'. *Journal of Immersion and Content-Based Language Education*, 6(2), 162–88.

Heyden, T. (2002). 'Shakespeare for ESL? *Hamlet* through Imaginative Writing'. *The Journal of the Imagination in Language Learning*, 7, 20–23.

Hill, W. F. & Öttchen, C. J. (1991). *Shakespeare's Insults: Educating Your Wit*. New York: Three Rivers Press.

Hill, W. F. & Öttchen, C. J. (1996). *Shakespeare's Insults for Teachers*. London: Clarkson Potter.

Holland, P. (2000). 'Modernizing Shakespeare: Nicholas Rowe and *The Tempest*'. *Shakespeare Quarterly*, 51(1), 24–32.

Horan, G. (2013). '"You Taught Me Language; and My Profit on't / Is, I Know How to Curse": Cursing and Swearing in Foreign Language Learning'. *Language and Intercultural Communication*, 13(3), 283–97.

Ibsen, E. B. (1990). 'The Double Role of Fiction in Foreign-Language Learning: Towards a Creative Methodology'. *English Teaching Forum*, 28(3), 2–9.

Ingram, M. (1994). '"Scolding Women Cucked or Washed": A Crisis in Gender Relations in Early Modern England?' In J. Kermode & G. Walker, eds., *Women, Crime and the Courts*. Chapel Hill: The University of North Carolina Press, pp. 48–80.

Ishihara, N. & Cohen, A. D. (2014). *Teaching and Learning Pragmatics: Where Language and Culture Meet*. London: Routledge.

Ivanova, I. (2018). 'Teachers' Perception of the Role of Pragmatics in the EFL Classroom'. *Studies in Linguistics, Culture and FLT*, 3, 27–44.

Jakobson, R. (1959). 'On Linguistic Aspects of Translation'. In R. A. Brower, ed., *On Translation*. Cambridge, MA: Harvard University Press, pp. 232–39.

Jucker, A. H., ed. (1995). *Historical Pragmatics: Pragmatic Developments in the History of English*. Amsterdam: John Benjamins.

Jucker, A. H. (1997). 'The Discourse Marker *Well* in the History of English'. *English Language & Linguistics*, 1(1), 91–110.

Jucker, A. H. (2002). 'Discourse Markers in Early Modern English'. In R. Watts & P. Trudgill, eds., *Alternative Histories of English*. London: Routledge, pp. 210–30.

Jucker, A. H. (2006). 'Historical Pragmatics'. In K. Brown, ed., *Encyclopedia of Language and Linguistics*. Oxford: Elsevier, pp. 329–32.

Jucker, A. H. & Taavitsainen, I. (2000). 'Diachronic Speech Act Analysis: Insults from Flyting to Flaming'. *Journal of Historical Pragmatics*, 1(1), 67–95.

Jucker, A. H. & Taavitsainen, I., eds. (2008). *Speech Acts in the History of English*. Amsterdam: John Benjamins.

Jucker, A. H. & Ziv, Y. (1998). 'Discourse Markers: Introduction'. In A. H. Jucker & Y. Ziv, eds., *Discourse Markers: Descriptions and Theory*. Amsterdam: John Benjamins, pp. 1–12.

Kaduce, R. & Metzger, N. (2019). 'Dagnabit! It's Time to Teach Swearing in ESL Classrooms'. *MIDTESOL Journal*, 2, 1–15.

Kapranov, O. (2018). 'Discourse Markers in the Genre of Formal Letters Written by Intermediate Students of English as a Foreign Language'. *Studies about Language*, 33, 74–89.

Kidnie, M. J. (2021). 'The Modern Editing of Shakespeare: The Text'. In L. Erne, ed., *The Arden Research Book of Shakespeare and Textual Studies*. London: The Arden Shakespeare Bloomsbury, pp. 188–205.

Kohnen, T. (2004). 'Methodological Problems in Corpus-Based Historical Pragmatics: The Case of English Directives'. In K. Aijmer &

B. Altenberg, eds., *Advances in Corpus Linguistics: Papers from the 23rd International Conference on English Language Research on Computerized Corpora (ICAME 23)*, Amsterdam: Rodopi, pp. 237–47.

Kohnen, T. (2008). 'Tracing Directives through Text and Time: Towards a Methodology of a Corpus-Based Diachronic Speech-Act Analysis'. In A. H. Jucker & I. Taavitsainen, eds., *Speech Acts in the History of English*. Amsterdam: John Benjamins, pp. 295–310.

Kohnen, T. (2015). 'Speech Acts: A Diachronic Perspective'. In K. Aijmer & C. Rühlemann, eds., *Corpus Pragmatics: A Handbook*. Cambridge: Cambridge University Press, pp. 52–83.

Kott, J. (1964). *Shakespeare Our Contemporary*, trans. B. Taborski. New York: Doubleday.

Krashen, S. (1978). 'The Monitor Model for Second Language Acquisition'. In R. C. Gingras, ed., *Second Language Acquisition and Foreign Language Teaching*. Arlington: Center for Applied Linguistics, pp. 1–26.

Kucharczyk, S. & Kucharczyk, M. (2022). *Teaching Shakespeare in Primary Schools: All the World's a Stage*. London: Routledge.

Labov, W. (1972). *Sociolinguistic Patterns*. Philadelphia: University of Pennsylvania Press.

Lachenicht, L. G. (1980). 'Aggravating Language: A Study of Abusing and Insulting Language'. *Paper in Linguistics*, 13(4), 607–88.

Lasagabaster, D. (2002). 'Towards an Interface of Language and Literature'. *Lenguaje y Textos*, 20, 21–34.

Lasagabaster, D. (2022). *English-Medium Instruction in Higher Education*. Cambridge: Cambridge University Press.

Lasagabaster, D. (2003). "Towards an Interface of Language and Literature." *Lenguaje y Textos*, 20, 21–34.

Lau, L. C. M. & Tso, W. B. A. (2017). *Teaching Shakespeare to ESL Students*. Singapore: Springer.

Leech, G. (1983). *Principles of Pragmatics*. London: Longman.

Lewis, D. (2011). 'A Discourse-Constructional Approach to the Emergence of Discourse Markers in English'. *Linguistics*, 49(2), 415–43.

Liyanage, I., Walker, T., Bartlett, B., & Guo, X. (2015). 'Accommodating Taboo Language in English Language Teaching: Issues of Appropriacy and Authenticity'. *Language, Culture and Curriculum*, 28(2), 113–25.

Llach, P. A. (2007). 'Teaching Language through Literature: *The Waste Land* in the ESL Classroom'. *Odisea*, 8, 7–17.

Lull, J., ed. (2009). *The New Cambridge Shakespeare: King Richard III*, updated ed. Cambridge: Cambridge University Press.

Lutzky, U. (2012). *Discourse Markers in Early Modern English*. Amsterdam: John Benjamins.

Lutzky, U. (2016). 'Exploring the Characterisation of Social Ranks in Early Modern English Comedies'. *Studies in Variation, Contacts and Change in English*, 17, https://varieng.helsinki.fi/series/volumes/17/lutzky/ [Accessed 16 February 2023].

Lyster, R. (2007). *Learning and Teaching Languages through Content: A Counterbalanced Approach*. Amsterdam: John Benjamins.

Lyster, R. (2018). *Content-Based Language Teaching*. New York: Routledge.

Macdonald, R. (2001). *Shakespeare and the Arts of Language*. Oxford: Oxford University Press.

Maley, A. (1989). 'Down from the Pedestal: Literature as Resource'. In R. Carter, R. Walker, & C. Brumfit, eds., *Literature and the Learner: Methodological Approaches*. Oxford: Modern English Publications in association with the British Council, pp. 10–24.

Maley, A. (2000). *Literature*, 9th ed. Oxford: Oxford University Press.

Malouf, A. (2017). '"Blame the Due of Blame": The Ethics and Efficacy of Curses in *Richard III*'. *Criterion: A Journal of Literary Criticism*, 10(1), 65–74.

Maschler, Y. (1994). 'Metalanguaging and Discourse Markers in Bilingual Conversation'. *Language in Society*, 23, 325–66.

Maschler, Y. (1998). '*Rotsè lishmoa kéta?* "Wanna Hear Something Weird/ Funny?" [Lit. "A Segment"]: Segmenting Israeli Hebrew Talk-in-Interaction'. In A. H. Jucker & Y. Ziv, eds., *Discourse Markers: Descriptions and Theory*. Amsterdam: John Benjamins, pp. 13–60.

Maschler, Y. & Schiffrin, D. (2015). 'Discourse Markers: Language, Meaning, and Context'. In D. Tannen, H. E. Hamilton, & D. Schiffrin, eds., *The Handbook of Discourse Analysis*, 2nd ed. Hoboken: John Wiley & Sons, pp. 54–75.

Maturi, M. (2021). '*Nulla è bene e male in sé, ma è il pensiero che lo rende tale*': *Analisi linguistica di parolacce e insulti nel teatro shakespeariano*. Unpublished BA thesis, Sapienza University of Rome.

Maune, J. F. (2015). 'Shakespeare's *Romeo and Juliet* in an EFL Life Science Course'. *Procedia – Social and Behavioral Sciences*, 171, 396–400.

Meiki, S. (2022). 'Learning Japanese Culture with Shakespeare'. *Okayama Economic Review*, 53(3), 81–88.

Mercury, R.-E. (1995). 'Swearing: A "Bad" Part of Language; A Good Part of Language Learning'. *TESL Canada Journal*, 13 (1), 28–36.

Molinelli, P. (2018). 'Different Sensitivity to Variation and Change: Italian Pragmatic Marker *Dai* vs. Discourse Marker *Allora*'. In S. Pons Bordería & O. Loureda Lamas, eds., *Beyond Grammaticalization and Discourse Markers: New Issues in the Study of Language Change*. Leiden: Brill, pp. 271–303.

Montini, D. (2013). 'Tracing Speech Acts through Text and Genre: Directives and Commissives in Queen Elizabeth I's Political Speeches and in Shakespeare's *Henry V*'. *Status Quaestionis*, 2(5), 130–46.

Mullini, R. (2016). 'The Pragmatics of Dialogical Asides in Shakespeare'. *Memoria di Shakespeare: A Journal of Shakespearean Studies*, 3, 69–81.

Murphy, S., Culpeper, J., Gillings, M., & Pace-Sigge, M. (2020). 'What Do Students Find Difficult When They Read Shakespeare? Problems and Solutions'. *Language and Literature*, 29(3), 302–26.

Nevalainen, T. (1999). 'Early Modern English Lexis and Semantics'. In R. Lass, ed., *The Cambridge History of the English Language*, vol. 3 (1476–1776). Cambridge: Cambridge University Press, pp. 332–458.

Nevalainen, T. (2006). *An Introduction to Early Modern English*. Edinburgh: Edinburgh University Press.

Novy, M. (2013). *Shakespeare and Outsiders*. Oxford: Oxford University Press.

Oliver, S. J. (2022). 'A Corpus-Based Approach to (Im)politeness Metalanguage: A Case Study on Shakespeare's Plays'. *Journal of Pragmatics*, 199, 6–20.

Orgel, S. (1996). *Impersonations: The Performance of Gender in Shakespeare's England*. Cambridge: Cambridge University Press.

Pecorari, D. & Malmström, H. (2018). 'At the Crossroads of TESOL and English Medium Instruction'. *TESOL Quarterly*, 52(3), 497–515.

Plag, I., Arndt-Lappe, S., Braun, M., & Schramm, M. (2015). *Introduction to English Linguistics*, 3rd ed. Berlin: de Gruyter.

Ponomareva, A. (2021). *The Application of Intersemiotic Translation in SLA*. Unpublished MA thesis, Sapienza University of Rome.

Reynolds, P. M. (2008). 'Mourning and Memory in *Richard III*'. *ANQ: A Quarterly Journal of Short Articles, Notes and Reviews*, 21(2), 19–25.

Romano, M. & Cuenca, M. J. (2013). 'Discourse Markers, Structure, and Emotionality in Oral Narratives'. *Narrative Inquiry*, 23(2), 344–70.

Sacks, H., Schegloff, E. A., & Jefferson, G. (1974). 'A Simplest Systematics for the Organization of Turn-Taking for Conversation'. *Language*, 50(4), 696–735.

Saltz, D. Z. (2000). 'The Reality of Doing: Real Speech Acts in the Theatre'. In D. Krasner, ed., *Method Acting Reconsidered: Theory, Practice, Future*. New York: Palgrave Macmillan, pp. 61–79.

Saner, E. (2023). 'OMG! Is Swearing Still a Taboo?' *The Guardian*, 2 September 2023, www.theguardian.com/science/2023/feb/09/is-swearing-still-taboo [Accessed 19 February 2023].

Savvidou, C. (2004). 'An Integrated Approach to the Teaching of Literature in the EFL Classroom'. *The Internet TESL Journal*, 10(12), 14–21 http://iteslj.org/Techniques/Savvidou-Literature.html#:~: text=An%20integrated%20approach%20to%20the,in%20all%20its%20dis course%20types [Accessed 26 July 2022].

Schalkwyk, D. (2019). 'The Performative Power of Shakespeare's Language'. In L. Magnusson & D. Schalkwyk, eds., *The Cambridge Companion to Shakespeare's Language*. Cambridge: Cambridge University Press, pp. 35–52.

Schiffrin, D. (1987). *Discourse Markers*. Cambridge: Cambridge University Press.

Schlieben-Lange, B. (1976). 'Für eine historische Analyse von Sprechakten'. In H. Weber & H. Weydt, eds., *Sprachtheorie und Pragmatik*. Tübingen: Niemeyer, pp. 113–19.

Schlieben-Lange, B. (1983). *Tradition des Sprechens: Elemente einer pragmatischen Sprachgeschichtsschreibung*. Stuttgart: Kohlhammer.

Schmidt, R. (1990). 'The Role of Consciousness in Second Language Learning'. *Applied Linguistics*, 11(2), 129–58.

Schourup, L. (1999). 'Discourse Markers: Tutorial Overview'. *Lingua*, 107, 227–65.

Searle, J. R. (1969). *Speech Acts: An Essay in the Philosophy of Language*. Cambridge: Cambridge University Press.

Sharif, M., Yarmohammadi, L., Sadighi, F., & Sadegh Bagheri, M. (2017). 'Teaching Pragmatics in the EFL Classroom: Challenges, Lacunas, and Suggestions'. *Advanced Education*, 8, 49–53.

Smith, R., ed. (2014). *Cambridge School Shakespeare: Romeo and Juliet*, 4th ed. Cambridge: Cambridge University Press.

Stein, D. (1985). 'Discourse Markers in Early Modern English'. In R. Eaton, O. Fischer, W. Koopman, & F. van der Leek, eds., *Papers from the Fourth International Conference on English Historical Linguistics*. Amsterdam: John Benjamins, pp. 283–302.

Stern, S. L. (1985). *Teaching Literature in ESL/EFL: An Integrative Approach*. Los Angeles: University of California Press.

Swan, S. (2013). 'Teaching Shakespearean Insults Helps My Students Decode the Bard's Language'. *The Guardian*, 24 April. www.theguardian.com/teacher-network/teacher-blog/2013/apr/24/shakespeare-lesson-ideas-teaching-insults [Accessed 13 March 2023].

Taavitsainen, I., Jucker, A. H., & Tuominen, J., eds. (2015). *Diachronic Corpus Pragmatics*. Amsterdam: John Benjamins.

Targoff, R. (2002). '"Dirty" Amens: Devotion, Applause, and Consent in *Richard III*'. *Renaissance Drama*, 31, 61–84.

Terkourafi, M. (2021). 'Inference and Implicature'. In M. Haugh & D. Z. Kádár, eds., *Cambridge Handbooks in Language and Linguistics*. Cambridge: Cambridge University Press, pp. 30–47.

Thom, N. T. T. (2008). 'Using Literary Texts in Language Teaching'. *VNU Journal of Science, Foreign Language*, 24, 120–26.

Thomas, K. (1971). *Religion and the Decline of Magic: Studies in Popular Beliefs in Sixteenth and Seventeenth Century England*. London: Weidenfeld and Nicolson.

Thompson, A., ed. (2017). *The New Cambridge Shakespeare: The Taming of the Shrew*, 3rd ed. Cambridge: Cambridge University Press.

Thompson, S. A. & Mulac, A. (1991). 'A Quantitative Perspective on the Grammaticization of Epistemic Parentheticals in English'. In E. C. Traugott & B. Heine, eds., *Approaches to Grammaticalization*, 2 vols. Amsterdam: John Benjamins, pp. 313–29.

Timucin, M. (2001). 'Gaining Insight into Alternative Teaching Approaches Employed in an EFL Literature Class'. *Revista de Filología y su Didáctica*, 24, 269–93.

Traugott, E. C. & Dasher, R. B. (2002). *Regularity in Semantic Change*. Cambridge: Cambridge University Press.

Tso, A. W. (2016). 'Teaching Shakespeare to Young ESL Learners in Hong Kong'. *Journal of Pedagogic Development*, 6(2), 18–24.

Uchimaru, K. (2020). '"Wisely, and Slow. They Stumble That Run Fast": Learner-Friendly Shakespeare in an EFL Classroom'. *Early Modern Culture Online*, 7, 66–86.

Underdown, D. E. (1985). 'The Taming of the Scold: The Enforcement of Patriarchal Authority in Early Modern England'. In A. Fletcher & J. Stevenson, eds., *Order and Disorder in Early Modern England*. Cambridge: Cambridge University Press, pp. 116–39.

Vaught, J. C. (2008). *Masculinity and Emotion in Early Modern English Literature*. Aldershot: Ashgate.

Verdonik, D. (2022). 'Annotating Dialogue Acts in Speech Data: Problematic Issues and Basic Dialogue Act Categories'. *International Journal of Corpus Linguistics: Online-First Articles*, doi.org/10.1075/ijcl.20165.ver [Accessed 13 January 2023].

Vienne-Guerrin, N. (2022). *The Anatomy of Insults in Shakespeare's World*. London: The Arden Shakespeare.

Vilches, M. L. (2001). 'Language and Literature: The Inseparable Interface'. *English Teacher: An International Journal*, 4(2), 136–46.

Vygotsky, L. (1978). 'Interaction between Learning and Development'. *Readings on the Development of Children*, 23(3), 34–41.

Wedlock, J. (2020). 'Teaching about Taboo Language in EFL/ESL Classes: A Starting Point'. *ORTESOL Journal*, 37, 33–47.

Weisser, M. (2016). 'DART – The Dialogue Annotation and Research Tool'. *Corpus Linguistics and Linguistic Theory*, 12(2), 355–88.

Weisser, M. (2018). *How to Do Corpus Pragmatics on Pragmatically Annotated Data: Speech Acts and Beyond*. Amsterdam: John Benjamins.

Weisser, M. (2019). 'The DART Annotation Scheme: Form, Applicability and Application'. *Studia Neophilologica*, 91(2), 131–53.

Weisser, M. (2020). 'Speech Acts in Corpus Pragmatics: Making the Case for an Extended Taxonomy'. *International Journal of Corpus Linguistics*, 25(4), 400–25.

Wellek, R. & Warren, A. (1956). *Theory of Literature*, 3rd ed. New York: Harcourt, Brace.

Wells, S., ed. (1984). *Re-editing Shakespeare for the Modern Reader*. Oxford: Oxford University Press.

White, G. (2015). 'How to Make Shakespeare Easy for English Language Learners'. *British Council*. 22 April. www.britishcouncil.org/voices-magazine/how-make-shakespeare-easy-english-language-learners [Accessed 13 March 2023].

Widdowson, H. G. (1975). *Stylistics and the Teaching Literature*. London: Longman.

Widdowson, H. G. (1978). *Teaching Language as Communication*. Oxford: Oxford University Press.

Wilson, D. (2016). 'Reassessing the Conceptual-Procedural Distinction'. *Lingua*, 175–76, 5–19.

Winston, J. & Tandy, M. (2012). *Beginning Shakespeare 4–11*. London: Routledge.

Yimwilai, S. (2015). 'An Integrated Approach to Teaching Literature in an EFL Classroom'. *English Language Teaching*, 8(2), 14–21.

Yule, G. (1996). *Pragmatics*. Oxford: Oxford University Press.

Zaroff, L. Z. (2010). 'Drowning in Science … Saved by Shakespeare: Teaching Literature to Premedical Students'. *Pharos Alpha Omega Alpha Honor Medical Society*, 73(2), 13–15.

Shakespeare and Pedagogy

Liam E. Semler
The University of Sydney

Liam E. Semler is Professor of Early Modern Literature in the Department of English at the University of Sydney. He is author of Teaching Shakespeare and Marlowe: Learning versus the System (2013) and co-editor (with Kate Flaherty and Penny Gay) of Teaching Shakespeare beyond the Centre: Australasian Perspectives (2013). He is editor of Coriolanus: A Critical Reader (2021) and co-editor (with Claire Hansen and Jackie Manuel) of Reimagining Shakespeare Education: Teaching and Learning through Collaboration (Cambridge, forthcoming). His most recent book outside Shakespeare studies is The Early Modern Grotesque: English Sources and Documents 1500–1700 (2019). Liam leads the Better Strangers project which hosts the open-access Shakespeare Reloaded website (shakespearereloaded.edu.au).

Gillian Woods
Birkbeck College, University of London

Gillian Woods is Reader in Renaissance Literature and Theatre at Birkbeck College, University of London. She is the author of Shakespeare's Unreformed Fictions (2013; joint winner of Shakespeare's Globe Book Award), Romeo and Juliet: A Reader's Guide to Essential Criticism (2012), and numerous articles about Renaissance drama. She is the co-editor (with Sarah Dustagheer) of Stage Directions and Shakespearean Theatre (2018). She is currently working on a new edition of

A Midsummer Night's Dream for Cambridge University Press,
as well as a Leverhulme-funded monograph about Renaissance
Theatricalities. As founding director of the Shakespeare
Teachers' Conversations, she runs a seminar series that brings
together university academics, school teachers and
educationalists from non-traditional sectors, and she regularly
runs workshops for schools.

ABOUT THE SERIES
The teaching and learning of Shakespeare around the world is
complex and changing. Elements in Shakespeare and Pedagogy
synthesises theory and practice, including provocative, original
pieces of research, as well as dynamic, practical engagements with
learning contexts.

Cambridge Elements ☰

Shakespeare and Pedagogy

The Pedagogy of Watching Shakespeare
Bethan Marshall, Myfanwy Edwards, and Charlotte Dixie

Teaching English as a Second Language with Shakespeare
Fabio Ciambella

A full series listing is available at: www.cambridge.org/ESPG